# DEATH FEIGNING
# BEETLES
## OF THE UNITED STATES AND MEXICO

STANLEY DEAN RIDER JR.

DEATH FEIGNING BEETLES
OF THE UNITED STATES AND MEXICO

Copyright © 2024 by Stanley Dean Rider Jr.
All rights reserved.

Front cover: *Asbolus mexicanus*, *Cryptoglossa variolosa*, *Cryptoglossa muricata*, *Asbolus verrucosus*, *Schizillus laticeps*, *Cryptoglossa infausta*, *Asbolus laevis* and the Kelso Dunes.

Back Cover: *Asbolus laevis* and *Asbolus verrucosus* in death feigning pose.

ISBN: 979-8-218-50939-2 (hardcover)
ISBN: 979-8-9915885-0-8 (paperback)

Published by Stanley Dean Rider Jr.
Fairborn, OH 45324, USA

*To my undead loved ones with six legs*

# Table of Contents

1. INTRODUCTION ..................................................................... 1
2. BEETLE TAXONOMY ............................................................. 2
   *Morphology and taxonomy* ................................................. 2
   *Beetle characteristics* ......................................................... 5
3. THE TRIBE CRYPTOGLOSSINI .............................................. 11
   *Anatomical features* ......................................................... 11
   *Life cycle* .......................................................................... 16
   *Geographical range* .......................................................... 22
   *Habitat* ............................................................................. 25
   *Adaptations to the environment* ...................................... 32
4. DEATH FEIGNING BEETLE SPECIES ..................................... 39
   4.1 KEY CHARACTERISTICS ..................................................... 39
      *Genus level characteristics* ............................................ 39
      *Species level characteristics* .......................................... 43
   4.2 SPECIES DESCRIPTIONS ..................................................... 47
      *Captive breeding data* ................................................... 47
      *Pronunciation respelling* ............................................... 47
      *Distribution map* ........................................................... 48
      *Original discovery* ......................................................... 49
      *Meaning of the scientific name* ..................................... 49
      *Unique features of the species* ...................................... 49
      *Photographs* .................................................................. 49
   4.2.1 ASBOLUS LAEVIS ............................................................ 50
   4.2.2 ASBOLUS MEXICANUS ..................................................... 51
   4.2.3 ASBOLUS PAPILLOSUS ..................................................... 52
   4.2.4 ASBOLUS VERRUCOSUS .................................................... 54
   4.2.5 CRYPTOGLOSSA ASPERATA ............................................... 55
   4.2.6 CRYPTOGLOSSA BICOSTATA .............................................. 56
   4.2.7 CRYPTOGLOSSA CARABOIDES ............................................ 57
   4.2.8 CRYPTOGLOSSA INFAUSTA ................................................ 58
   4.2.9 CRYPTOGLOSSA MICHELBACHERI ....................................... 60
   4.2.10 CRYPTOGLOSSA MURICATA .............................................. 60
   4.2.11 CRYPTOGLOSSA SERIATA ................................................. 62

4.2.12 CRYPTOGLOSSA SPICULIFERA ........................................................ 63
4.2.13 CRYPTOGLOSSA VARIOLOSA ......................................................... 65
4.2.14 SCHIZILLUS LATICEPS .................................................................. 66
4.2.15 SCHIZILLUS NUNENMACHERI ........................................................ 67
4.3 CHEAT SHEETS ................................................................................ 69
    Cheat sheet for Schizillus species ................................................. 69
    Cheat sheet for Asbolus species ................................................... 69
    Cheat sheet for Cryptoglossa species .......................................... 70

## 5. THE BESTEST PETS ........................................................................ 71

    Obtaining beetles ........................................................................... 72
    Housing ........................................................................................... 75
    Food and water .............................................................................. 78
    Death Feigning behavior ............................................................... 81
    Decorating beetles ......................................................................... 81
    Longevity ........................................................................................ 88
    Parasites and diseases .................................................................. 90

## 6. ADVANCED TECHNIQUES ............................................................... 95

    Sex Determination ......................................................................... 96
    Containers .................................................................................... 105
    Sand and coconuts ...................................................................... 108
    Half in ........................................................................................... 108
    Stratifying immatures .................................................................. 111
    Organic substrates ....................................................................... 115
    Clay ............................................................................................... 118
    Water ............................................................................................ 123
    Food .............................................................................................. 128
    Incubators .................................................................................... 132
    Humidity ....................................................................................... 134
    Sterilizing materials ..................................................................... 136

## 7. CAPTIVE BREEDING ...................................................................... 141

7.1 THE ORIGINAL '14 RECIPE ............................................................. 141
7.2 STANDARDIZED METHODS ............................................................. 141
    Standard substrate ...................................................................... 141
    Standard diet ................................................................................ 142
    Standard temperature ................................................................. 142
    Standard relative humidity (RH) ................................................. 142
7.3 DETAILED INSTRUCTIONS .............................................................. 142

Eggs ................................................................................... 142
First instar larvae .............................................................. 143
2nd to 5th instar larvae .................................................... 143
Maturing larvae (instars 5-9+) ......................................... 143
Pupae ................................................................................ 144
Young beetles ................................................................... 144
Environmentally hardened beetles ................................. 145

## 8. CITIZEN SCIENCE .................................................... 145

Improved rearing .............................................................. 147
Missing life stages ............................................................ 147
Lifespan studies ................................................................ 149
Behavioral studies ............................................................ 149
Population studies ............................................................ 150
Where do they hide? ........................................................ 150

## 9. EPILOGUE ................................................................. 151

## 10. RESOURCES ............................................................ 153

Beetle Sources .................................................................. 153
Substrate Mixes ................................................................ 153
Containers ......................................................................... 154
Incubator Kits ................................................................... 154
Large Incubators .............................................................. 154
Aquariums ......................................................................... 155
Heatlamps ......................................................................... 155
Tiny plants ........................................................................ 155
Useful terms ..................................................................... 156

# PREFACE

I kept bugs as pets for decades. Then a pointed remark by my brother sent me on a quest. He said that the pet beetles (superworms) in my living room display tank were not very colorful. I needed to find a good pet beetle that was colorful and easy to care for. A giant ladybug that eats dog chow would have been impressive. When I came across blue death feigning beetles for sale online, I was hooked. Death feigning beetles are prized as pets, displayed in zoos, and used for group outreach programs. They are amazing!

My first blue death feigning beetles were a Valentine's Day gift from my late wife. This was to be my starter culture. There was just one problem: captive breeding of blue death feigning beetles had never been done. Only two species of death feigning beetles had been induced to complete their life cycle in captivity - in a laboratory at Ohio State University.

The consensus among hobbyists was that blue death feigning beetles could not be bred in captivity. A lot of effort and experimentation over an eight-month period ensued. Then I discovered what was needed for blue death feigning beetles to complete their life cycle. My breakthrough discovery got a lot of people excited online. I had numerous requests for a clear recipe. Therefore, a good portion of this book is dedicated to captive breeding and the care of immature stages of the beetles.

Other hobbyists have inspired modifications. Debates covered the best methods to use. Discussions took place in emails and online posts. Several new species have been added to the captive rearing success stories within the hobby. I have tracked those rearing tweaks over the years while lurking online in the least nefarious way possible. Rearing beetles is a subject of continued growth in the field of entomology. It is not just for hobbyists. The immature stages of hundreds of thousands of insect species have never been described. Perhaps some readers will pursue beetle breeding and add to the body of scientific knowledge in a meaningful way. There is very little to stop you from doing so ...

especially if you live where insect breeding seems to be less regulated and more highly esteemed.

Why, in this age, make a book about these bugs? Because, I love books about bugs. There is some nostalgia involved. I used to crawl under cars with the neighbor kid. We would pull dead bugs off the grilles and bumpers to add new bugs to our collections. My dad would also take me to the countryside to hunt bugs along the roadsides. We would try to identify them using books borrowed from the town library.

I enjoyed the species distribution maps in the field guides. Those maps made me dream of visiting the places where the more exotic creatures lived. Eventually, I did. I had hopes of finding these treasures and adding them to my collection.

My favorite books used photographs of live insects in their natural habitat (or at least specimens posed to look natural). Full color photographs had more impact on me at a young age than line drawings. I was fortunate to have some amazing wildlife photographers provide some of their best photographs for use in this book.

This book is intended for people who like bugs ... especially keeping pet bugs. It is great for people who prefer to be informed by pictures. It also has sections available for those who have grown to a more advanced level. It is made for those who do not want to spend countless hours online or in the library to compile the information presented in this book. This is the book I wish I had when I started. I hope you enjoy this book. I hope you learn something useful and something new.

-Dean Rider

## ACKNOWLEDGEMENTS

A generous set of individuals who spend their time and resources dedicated to exploring nature helped to make this book possible. Some have allowed their photographs to be included, while others provided specimens. I would like to highlight the following individuals for their contributions:

### Photographs (in order of appearance)
*Cryptoglossa muricata* photo by Tristan Shanahan
*Asbolus papillosus* photos by Hartmut Wisch
*Cryptoglossa asperata* photo by Steven Mlodinow
*Cryptoglossa bicostata* photo by Barry Sullender
*Cryptoglossa seriata* photo by Álvaro San José Elizundia
*Cryptoglossa spiculifera* photos by Robin Gwen Agarwal
*Schizillus nunenmacheri* photo by Vahe Martirosyan
Decorative enclosure photo by French J. Damewood IV
Tachinid photo by Salvador Vitanza
Parasitized *Cryptoglossa asperata* photo by Ana Gatica-Colima

### Specimens (in order of appearance)
*Asbolus* specimens from Tristan Shanahan
*Schizillus* specimens from Peter Clausen

# 1. INTRODUCTION

It is no surprise that death feigning beetles are popular. They are among the most active and curious beetles I've kept. That is, when they were not playing dead! Internet searches for death feigning beetles jumped almost 4× after 2016. That was the year I posted a short video online sharing the secret to raising these beetles in captivity! Is the rise in interest a mere coincidence?

By 2020, YouTubers showed that captive breeding worked for them too. The internet searches then exploded to 10× what they were before 2016. They have now increased to over 30×! Blue death feigning beetles are more popular than ever. They have been called the best invertebrate! I hope even more people come to appreciate these beautiful and entertaining insects.

The blue death feigning beetle is just one of fifteen death feigning beetle species. This book covers them all. This book aims to encourage new beetle lovers and at the same time provide value to informed enthusiasts. If you don't know much about beetles, that's great! This book is part field guide and part pet care manual. You'll get everything you need to know to identify all the death feigning beetle species and how to keep them as pets.

If you had a blue death feigning beetle in your hand, it might be obvious what it is. But why is it obvious? How do we formally define what a blue death feigning beetle is? What are its parts? How do they differ from other related beetles? The overarching goal in these early chapters is to answer those questions and more.

The first few chapters introduce about 80 important beetle-related words and concepts. These are in bold type. The new lingo swings into action and the story builds on itself. If you follow along - in step with the book, you won't get lost. Pictures might come a little before or after the text, but they are there to help.

The purpose of these early chapters is to review the basics and get everybody on the same page. The nice thing is that you have this book, so you can always come back to it as a reference.

If you already know a lot about beetles, that's great too! This book starts at a basic level and rapidly dives deeply into more sophisticated areas of morphology. The later chapters get pretty technical. They will provide a roadmap for solving problems with raising beetles in captivity. How do they complete their life cycle? Where do they live? What do they eat? What techniques are working? What do we need to test? Where are there gaps in our knowledge? There is still a lot about these critters that we don't know. Maybe you'll want to try a few experiments and help others improve their techniques.

There are a lot of questions here, and I am eager to share the answers with you. So, let's talk about beetles!

# 2. BEETLE TAXONOMY

If you take a random sample of the animals of earth, there is a good chance that the animal you collect first is a beetle. Insects represent the most diverse class of animals on the planet. Insects are 75% of all animal species. Beetles are a wonderful mix of creatures that make up about 40% of the insect species. People generally accept that beetles are the largest group of organisms on the planet. Thus, there is a good chance that you will come across a beetle sooner, rather than later. But what counts as a beetle and how do we know?

## Morphology and taxonomy

To separate beetles from the other life forms, we need to use **morphology** - key physical characters. Each key character is going to help divide organisms into separate groups, so we can classify them. **Taxonomy** is the classification of living organisms into ranked groups. The ranking gets more specific as we eliminate some organisms from the list and keep others. Let's take a look at how that works.

The rank of kingdom is the highest rank used here. Plants, animals and fungi are three of the kingdoms. We can usually see these without a microscope. The other remaining kingdoms cover

**Figure 2.1**
Examples of arthropods that are not beetles.

**Figure 2.2**
Examples of insects that are beetles.

microscopic organisms. Unlike plants and fungi, animals are able to move. So, we are looking at some pretty diverse organisms at the kingdom level. When we start with organisms we recognize as animals, we put them in the **kingdom Animalia**.

Animals that have exoskeletons belong to the **phylum Arthropoda**. This includes things like crabs, lobsters, centipedes, scorpions, spiders and insects. It does not include birds, reptiles, mammals, or amphibians. It does not include worms, snails, squid, sponges or any of the other animals. It is a pretty selective group. Six-legged arthropods (**subphylum Hexapoda**), include the insects (**class Insecta**).

> **BEETLE TAXONOMY**
> **kindgom** Animalia - animals
> **phylum** Arthropoda - arthropods
> **subphylum** Hexapoda - hexapods
> **class** Insecta - insects
> **order** Coleoptera - beetles

There are many animals that are not arthropods. There are many arthropods that have more than six legs. There are some hexapod critters that aren't insects! Can you see how each rank of the taxonomy separates things into more refined groups based on a small number of physical characteristics? We can keep doing this all the way down to the species level, which is our goal.

## Beetle characteristics

Just a few characters separated the insects from all the other animals. Adult insects usually have three recognizable body regions. The regions include the **head**, the **thorax**, and the **abdomen**. The head (as you may know) is basically the front of the bug. It is the place where bugs take in food and sense their environment. The main thing is that the head has various appendages, including eyes and antennae.

We are now going to move back along the body. It is a good time to introduce the words anterior and posterior. **"Anterior"** is toward the head. **"Posterior"** is toward the other end. Moving

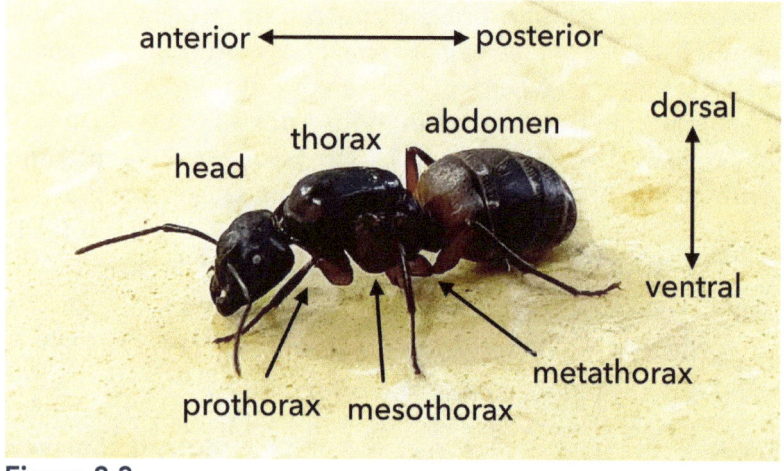

**Figure 2.3**
This ant represents a typical insect body plan. The head, thorax and abdomen are labeled. The three sections of the thorax are labeled. Directions for anterior, posterior, dorsal and ventral are also shown.

from the head towards the posterior end, the next part is the thorax. The thorax is where the legs and wings are attached. The thorax regulates locomotion. Now is a good time to introduce dorsal and ventral. "**Dorsal**" is the back or upwards for most bugs. "**Ventral**" is the equivalent of the stomach or downward side if you were crawling on the ground. Dorsal and ventral define directions. We call the ventral side of the bug the "**sternum**". The segments on the sternum are called **"sternites"**. Wings are more dorsal appendages. Legs are more ventral. Moving toward the posterior from the thorax is the abdomen. The wings of insects often cover the abdomen. At this point, nothing is clearly "beetle-like".

We know insects are divided into three main body parts. But the main body parts of beetles can be difficult to distinguish. This is because a lot of fusion or compaction occurs among various forms. Fortunately, death feigning beetles have some distinct body regions if you look at them on the dorsal surface. For example, it is easy for us to identify the head. The head of the beetle bears many appendages. These include the **mouthparts**,

**eyes**, and **antennae**. You can't see the mouthparts of a death feigning beetle very well from the dorsal side. They are hidden. The eyes and antennae have important features used for identification purposes. The eyes are multi-faceted. We call each facet in a death feigning beetle's eye an **"ommatidium"** (plural = ommatidia).

**Figure 2.4**
Compound eye from a death feigning beetle. The circular facets are ommatidia.

The number of ommatidia at certain locations in the eye is helpful in separating death feigning beetles into three major groups. The text will cover this in Chapter 4. Once we identify those groups, we can then separate beetles into individual species.

Multiple segments make up the antennae. The numbering or counting of the segments starts where the antenna is attached to the head. For at least two species of death feigning beetle, the relative length of specific antennal segments is used to separate one species from the other. The text will cover this in Chapter 4 as well.

The dorsal part of the thorax is called the **"notum"**. The thorax is made of multiple segments. Because they are somewhat fused together and fused to the abdomen, they are more difficult to distinguish. The three parts going from anterior to posterior are the **prothorax**, the **mesothorax** and the **metathorax**. We name some body parts with the prefixes "pro-", "meso-", or "meta-" to indicate which thoracic segment they belong to. It is shorter to write "pronotum" than to write "the notum of the prothorax". Each thoracic segment possesses a pair of legs. The mesothorax and metathorax also may possess wings.

The **pronotum** is the next visible section of a death feigning beetle. The mesothorax of death feigning beetles has wings. This

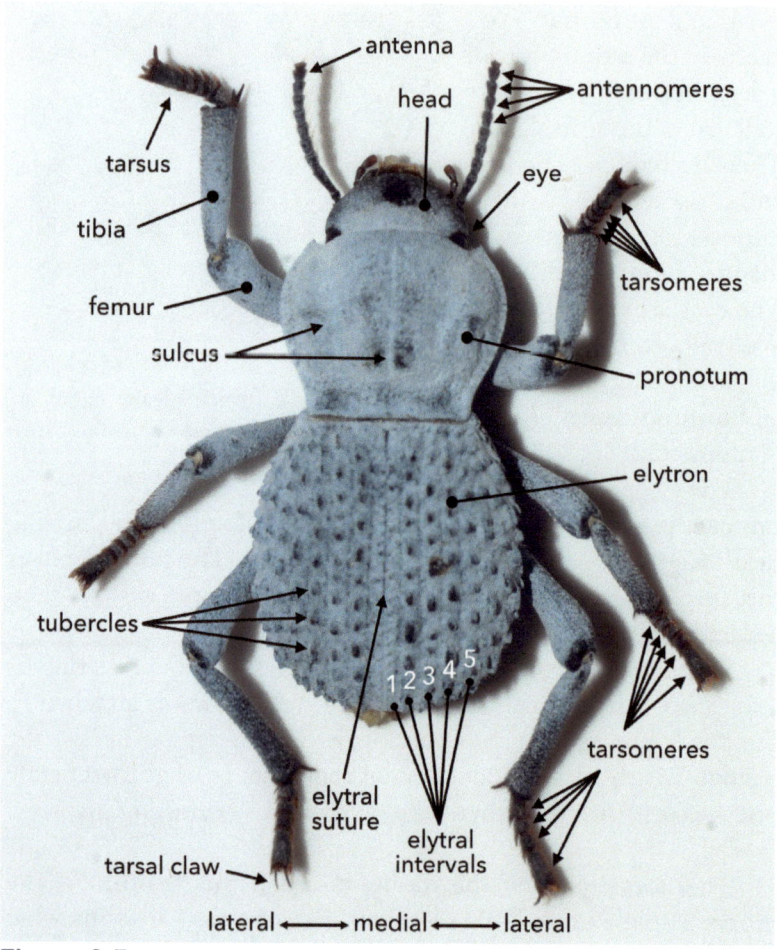

**Figure 2.5**
Parts of a beetle when viewed from the dorsal side.

is where unique beetle-like characteristics begin to emerge. Does it have wings that form a hard shell? Do those wings meet in a straight line running down the dorsal side of the bug? If you answered yes to those two questions, then your bug has a good chance of being a beetle. This is the **order Coleoptera**.

Those hardened or leathery wings of beetles are **elytra** (singular = elytron). Elytra cover the remainder of the body - including the rest of the thorax and the abdomen. You cannot see

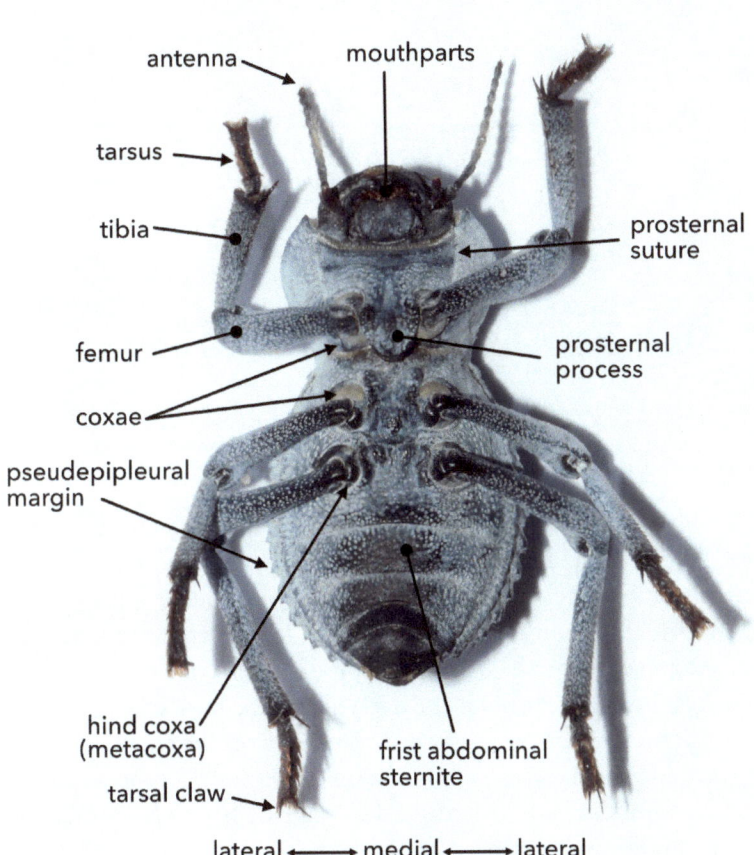

**Figure 2.6**
Parts of a beetle when viewed from the ventral side.

most of the dorsal side of the thorax because of the elytra. Elytra are the third visible section of a death feigning beetle when viewed from above. That line that runs between the elytra is the **elytral suture**. You may notice that the text uses the word "bug" to mean insect. Bravo for you! Technically, bugs are insects, but not all insects are bugs. However, these terms will be used interchangeably in this text... even though we know better!

We covered the sections of the beetle. We know that the head, pronotum and elytra are the main parts visible from the dorsal

**Figure 2.7**

Insects in the order Hemiptera have wings that criss-cross and form a large triangle behind the pronotum. These are the only group we can correctly call "bugs". They are often confused with beetles.

view. The text mentioned that some parts are invisible from the dorsal view. What about the underside? What can we see from the ventral view? When you flip a death feigning beetle on its back, we can see the mouthparts much better. Each pair of legs defines a thoracic segment that you can see on the ventral side. Those segments become more clear once you realize they exist.

One feature that is important to note is on the prothorax and on the ventral side. It is an interesting projection that lies near the center of the beetle between the first pair of legs. The projection that extends toward the posterior between the legs is called the **"prosternal process"**. The absence of a prosternal process uniquely identifies one species of death feigning beetles.

When a feature is near the middle of the insect, this is referred to as **"medial"**. As you move from the midline toward either the left or right, we refer to this direction as **"lateral"**. This is important. Some features of the elytra and pronotum may be more or less medial, or they may be more or less lateral in their location.

The morphology of the legs is important when you want to identify certain species. Legs also are used to determine the sex of many of the death feigning beetle species. The more distinct regions include the **femur**, the **tibia**, and the **tarsus**. Looking at the legs from the ventral side reveals additional features. The **coxa** (plural = coxae), for example, is the segment that connects the leg to the body.

Although hidden from above, nine or ten segments make up the abdomen. Many abdominal segments are not visible from the ventral side. We don't use abdominal features to identify individual death feigning beetle species. We also don't use them for sex determination. Abdominal features are key to determining higher and lower level taxonomic groupings such as subspecies.

---

Section Summary
- Taxonomy is based on how things look (it is based on morphology)
- Taxonomy puts organisms into ranked categories
- The class Insecta has these characteristics:
    - three body regions (head, thorax, abdomen)
    - six legs
    - antennae
- The word "bug" refers to insects in the order Hemiptera but the term is often used to mean any insect-like critter
- Coleoptera (the beetles) are insects with hard front wings meeting in a straight line down the back

---

# 3. THE TRIBE CRYPTOGLOSSINI

## Anatomical features

The previous section was about characteristics that define a beetle. We went through questions that had a yes or no type of answer. That is the basis of taxonomy. We needed to look at key morphological details. This required some new vocabulary. The

> **DEATH FEIGNING BEETLE TAXONOMY**
> **order** Coleoptera - beetles
>   **suborder** Polyphaga
>     **superfamily** Tenebrionoidea
>       **family** Tenebrionidae - darklings
>         **subfamily** Pimeliinae
>           **tribe** Cryptoglossini - death feigning beetles

same is true for identifying species. We will continue the same method in this chapter and part of the next. We can ask a series of questions as we go down the path. Each question splits organisms into more refined groups. We look at more detailed characteristics until we can identify an individual to the species level. Between the order "Coleoptera" and the tribe "Cryptoglossini" are many steps.

Can you see if the hind coxa (**metacoxa**) passes beyond the first abdominal segment? If so, then we want to ignore those beetles. If the metacoxa does not pass beyond the first abdominal segment, that is the group we want. You should look at the metacoxa in figure 2.6. That is a good example of what to look for. You can look back at figures 2.5 and 2.6 as we go over the other key features.

If the beetle lacks **notopleural sutures**, then we keep it. Notopleural sutures are present only on water beetles and ground beetles. You can see what one looks like in figure 3.1. It is important to be aware of this feature in these groups to rule them out. The group that lacks notopleural sutures is the **suborder Polyphaga**. The suborder Polyphaga is a diverse group. It includes some of the largest beetles in the world. Giants like the Goliath beetle, Titan beetle and Hercules beetle are in this group. Polyphaga includes the more adorable beetles like ladybugs and fireflies too. While death feigning beetles are impressive in their own right, they are not that closely related to the beetles mentioned above. Does it have **prosternal sutures**? Does it have

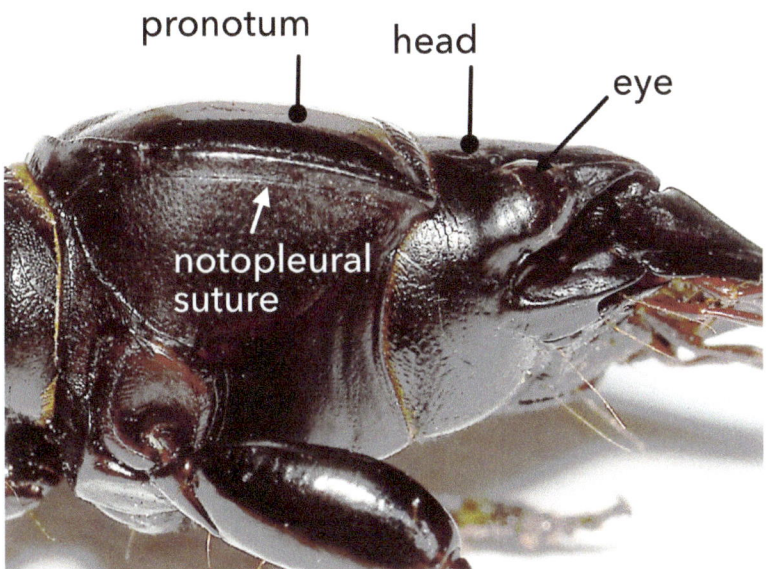

**Figure 3.1**
Notopleural suture on a ground beetle prothorax.

elytra that completely cover the abdomen? If so, you are getting closer!

We need to ask important questions about the number of segments in the antennae and the segments that make up the final parts of the legs. The antennae must have eleven antennal segments (**"antennomeres"**). Can you tell if it has eleven? The first one is in a groove and the second one is very short. The last segment has to be shorter than the others. You should be able to see that the last segment is smaller than the others! In death feigning beetles, the last antennomere is very small.

Multiple segments called **"tarsomeres"** make up the feet (**tarsi**) of insects. You should see 5 tarsomeres on the front and middle legs. The metatarsi must have 4 tarsomeres. Beetle enthusiasts call this the **"5-5-4 tarsal formula"**. The tarsal claws must be smooth and without teeth. We call this "pectinate" when teeth are present. Are the eyes interrupted by a notch? If yes, this combination of characters strongly suggests the beetle is in the **family Tenebrionidae**.

The name is derived from the Latin word "tenebrio" which translates to "one who shuns light" or "lover of darkness". As the name suggests, most darkling beetles love to find dark places to hide during the daytime. In addition, they are often dark-colored, being black or brown.

You can shorten the family name to "tenebs". This sounds like "10 ebbs". Tenebs are also known as **darkling beetles**. The darkling beetle family is a group of nearly 30,000 species worldwide. There are over 2,000 species in North America. Tenebrionids are among the largest and most conspicuous beetles in the USA and Mexico. They also include some serious pests like the red flour beetle and mealworm beetles.

Further divisions within Tenebrionidae become difficult. This is because different lineages lose or gain some important characteristics. The separation of tenebrionids into subfamilies and tribes is best left to the experts. Many key questions involve internal female reproductive structures and the morphology of immature stages. Scientists are resolving some questions with the taxonomy using DNA-based methods.

However, no matter how hard you look on the exterior of an adult beetle, you will not find any stink glands. In the **subfamily Pimeliinae** none of the beetles possess stink glands. So, if you capture a suspected death feigning beetle, and it stinks up the place or stains your skin, it is not a death feigning beetle or even a close relative! The **tribe Cryptoglossini** is a group within the Pimeliinae.

The mouthparts of the Cryptoglossini are hard to see from the dorsal view. The tribe name comes from the Greek *kruptos* meaning "hidden" and *glossa* for "tongue". Thus, the tribe name means "hidden tongue". Within the tribe, there are three subgroups. Each of the subgroups is called a **genus** (plural = genera). The fifteen species of death feigning beetles all are placed within those three genera.

## DEATH FEIGNING BEETLE TAXONOMY

**tribe** Cryptoglossini
  **genus** *Asbolus*
    **species** *Asbolus laevis*
    **species** *Asbolus mexicanus*
    **species** *Asbolus papillosus*
    **species** *Asbolus verrucosus*
  **genus** *Cryptoglossa*
    **species** *Cryptoglossa asperata*
    **species** *Cryptoglossa bicostata*
    **species** *Cryptoglossa caraboides*
    **species** *Cryptoglossa infausta*
    **species** *Cryptoglossa michelbacheri*
    **species** *Cryptoglossa muricata*
    **species** *Cryptoglossa seriata*
    **species** *Cryptoglossa spiculifera*
    **species** *Cryptoglossa variolosa*
  **genus** *Schizillus*
    **species** *Schizillus laticeps*
    **species** *Schizillus nunenmacheri*

**Figure 3.2**
Mating behavior (mounting and copulation) in *Asbolus verrucosus*.

You may feel you are currently missing some things the experts use for identification. This doesn't mean that you can't make an expert-level guess. Once you become familiar with death feigning beetles, you will find them to be unmistakable... even without looking at the key features mentioned above. In the next chapter, all the species' unique characteristics will be described.

## Life cycle

We focused above on adult beetles. Before we go deeper into death feigning beetle taxonomy, you should know a little about the beetle life cycle and where they live. Being familiar with these things will help you understand each species a little better. The species descriptions cover unique physical characteristics as well as habitat preferences. All of this is helpful if you decide to go hunting for these guys in the wild.

Many bugs hatch from **eggs** looking like miniature versions of their adult selves. Beetles do not. Death feigning beetles lay eggs. In comparison to their body size, the eggs are quite large

**Figure 3.3**
Blue death feigning beetle female during (left) and after (right) egg laying.

(several millimeters or ⅛ inch long). A female death feigning beetle may have up to 4 dozen eggs inside her. The eggs are at different stages of development. She may lay about three eggs per day, usually a little after dusk. In captivity, they often stop laying eggs in winter. Eggs often have sand attached to them.

For the species that we can breed in captivity, we know it takes about two weeks for eggs to hatch. The egg hatches into a fat little grub-like **larva**. Sometimes people call this grub-like hatchling a larvula. More commonly we just call it a larva. This little baby worm may not feed for a while, possibly not until it molts. We call each stage of the worm an **instar**. After about a week or so, the first instar larva will molt into a more wiry second instar larva. Wiry larvae that look like worms are referred to as elateriform larvae. The reference comes from the larvae of click beetles (family Elateridae). We call click beetle larvae "wireworms". Death feigning beetle larvae are effectively desert mealworms. However, the occasional haughty entomologist will correct you and point out that mealworms are the larvae of specific beetles that infest grain. These include the yellow, dark and lesser mealworms. Tenebrionid larvae are also known as **false wireworms**.

Second instar larvae definitely eat. The larvae eat and grow and molt 5 times or more until they are about 1.75 inches long (4.4 cm). The body length does not matter as much as the width of the head. The body length is variable, depending on if they are moving, playing dead, well-fed etc. However, the exoskeleton of

**Figure 3.4**

Eggs of *Asbolus verrucosus, Cryptoglossa muricata, Cryptoglossa variolosa* (left panel) and a first instar blue death feigning beetle larva (right panel).

the head is pretty much hardened and cannot stretch like the body can. So, it is the width of the **head capsule** that matters most when determining the age or instar of the larva. This growing stage takes about three months. Mature larvae for the blue death feigning beetle and its relatives have head capsules that are about 3 millimeters in width (⅛ inch). At this stage, they are mature.

Depending on the species, the larvae may be very good at playing dead when disturbed. The larvae of the blue death feigning beetle are pretty good at this. The others don't seem to be as good at it. Some larvae play dead so hard that they literally squeeze until they pop. When this happens, a tiny bit of blood may squirt out. We call insect blood **"hemolymph"**. The bloody body gets camouflaged with sand. This may help the larvae hide from lizards and other animals that are looking for something to eat! Another defense that the larvae show is rapid wriggling. This probably helps them to escape some weaker predators and probably helps fight cannibalism. If the larva makes it to the size where they are ready to become a beetle, they may wander. Wandering means they are running around looking for a better place to become a beetle.

The larvae will tunnel deep into the soil and form an oval space. They then curl up into a C-shape and wait for the proper signals to molt. They will molt into an intermediate stage between

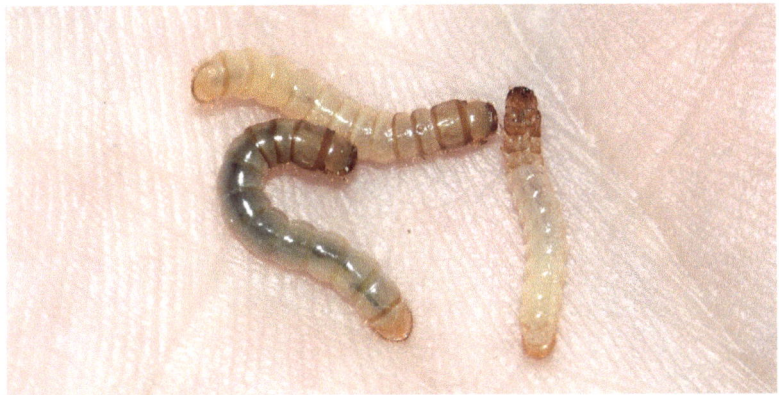

**Figure 3.5**
Young death feigning beetle larvae. The one to the right is playing dead.

**Figure 3.6**
Mature blue death feigning beetle larva.

larva and adult beetle. This intermediate stage is a **pupa** (plural = pupae). Sometimes people call the C-shape stage a **pre-pupa**. The little space they make for themselves is a **pupal cell**. For several death feigning beetle species, an increase in temperature signals the larva to pupate. It takes several weeks for the high heat to take effect. We can divide the pupae of insects into two categories: exarate and obtect. **Exarate pupae** have their legs and wings loose or free from the body. **Obtect pupae** have their appendages sealed inside or attached to the body. A butterfly chrysalis is a good example of an obtect pupa. Death feigning beetles have exarate pupae. They can move but not walk.

**Figure 3.7**
Young pupa inside a pupal cell.

On the surface of their thorax and abdomen, near the lateral edges, are tiny tooth-like points. These differ between species. The places where two sets of pointy edges can come together and "bite" a potential attacker are called **"gin traps"**. So, just like the larvae, pupae wriggle to protect themselves. The pupae are cream-colored except for the tips of the gin traps, which are light brown.

The shape of the thorax and eyes are like the adult forms. You can get a rough idea of which species of pupa you have from these features. As the pupa matures, the tips of the tarsi, mouthparts and eyes begin to darken. It takes only about two weeks for a pupa to mature and molt to become an adult beetle. The final molting process from pupa to adult is **"eclosion"**. Adults are about ¾ inch (~19 millimeters) long.

Freshly eclosed adult beetles are fragile and are not yet considered mature. They are pale cream-colored except for a few places. Death feigning beetles remain motionless most of the time for at least a few days following the molt to adulthood.

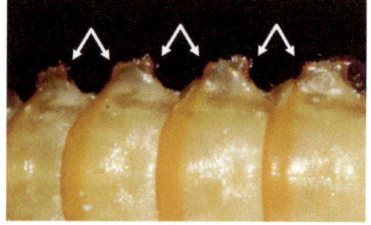

**Figure 3.8**
Gin traps on the dorsal surface of a tenebrionid pupa. Arrows show sets of pointy edges.

**Figure 3.9**
Older pupa near time of eclosion.

**Figure 3.10**
Teneral adults. Top left - *Cryptoglossa muricata*. Top right - *Asbolus laevis*. Bottom left - *Asbolus verrucosus*. Bottom right - *Asbolus mexicanus mexicanus*. *Cryptoglossa muricata* photo by Tristan Shanahan. *Asbolus* photos by S. Dean Rider Jr. *Asbolus mexicanus mexicanus* specimen from Tristan Shanahan.

They very slowly turn a rusty brown color. They eventually turn blackish and finally begin to secrete any waxy materials. The wax will change their surface colors from black to what you see in their mature adult stage. The immature adult stage, between when the beetles eclose and when they are looking completely like their adult form, is called a **"teneral adult"**. The adult beetle may lay inside its pupal cell for weeks, mostly laying on its back. Eventually, they will flip themselves over and stand up. Sometimes they stay in this position for many days. Once the beetle is past this stage, it will begin to dig its way out of the pupal cell to make its way to the surface. Even after they exhume themselves, they still may have a period of time before they eat or are ready to reproduce. The beetle life cycle takes many months but can be completed in under a year.

### Geographical range

Some species of death feigning beetles occupy a small territory, while others inhabit a very wide territory. Others live in multiple fragmented areas. These geographical ranges can help with species identification.

The death feigning beetle distributions came from three sources. First is Dr. Rolf Aalbu's manuscripts listing where people found museum specimens. Second is the Bugguide.net. Third is iNaturalist.com. Two species are unique to the USA. Five are unique to Mexico. Eight live in both countries. There is good agreement between the museum specimen locations and the photos posted on the internet.

You can use the distribution map presented here in two ways. First, you can see the states where death feigning beetles live because they are pink. Second, you can see the approximate locations for the species distributions because they are blue. This combination allows you to rapidly orient the geographic distribution of these beetles within territorial boundaries. An immediate reaction to this distribution map is that these beetles appear to be desert creatures. That is, in most cases, correct.

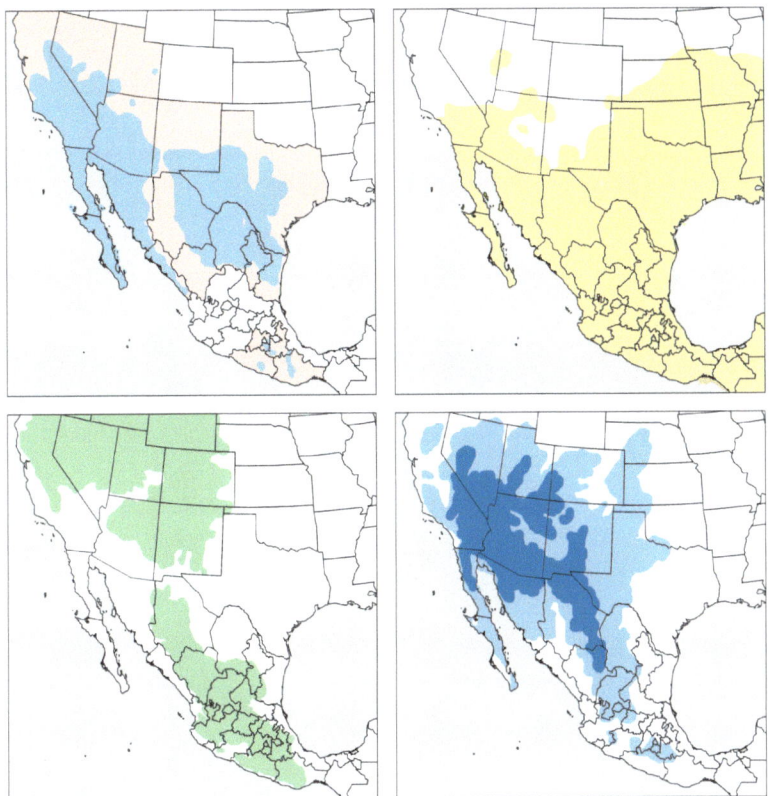

**Figure 3.11**

*Cryptoglossini* distribution map (top left), elevated temperatures (top right), higher altitude regions (bottom left) and low humidity regions (bottom right).

The distribution of this group of beetles correlates well with environmental factors. The factors include temperature, humidity and elevation. For example, these beetles seem to be restricted to places where the average temperatures are above 70°F (20°C). You can see these regions on the map in Figure 3.11 displaying warmer regions in gold. However, the warm regions do not represent the entire story. Most of the south-central and south-eastern USA is relatively warm. There are also large regions of Mexico where

**Figure 3.12**

Geographical regions of relevance to death feigning beetle distribution include the Great Basin, Mojave, Sonoran, Baja California, and Chihuahua deserts, the Gulf of California, the Sierra Madre Occidental Pine-Oak forest, and the Isthmus of Tehuantepec.

nobody finds these beetles... despite the relatively warmer temperatures.

Interestingly, a striking correlation is that of elevation. No one normally finds these beetles in places that are ~1500 meters (4900 feet) or more above sea level. We can see these high elevation regions in green on the elevation map. High elevation seems to represent a barrier to most species of death feigning beetles. Again, this story is somewhat incomplete. There are low-lying areas that are also warm but that do not seem to allow death feigning beetles to thrive. The last restriction seems to be related to humidity.

These beetles are restricted to the drier regions of North America. The map of low humidity shows areas where the average annual relative humidity is below 50 percent in light blue. It also shows the regions that are less than 45 percent humidity in darker blue. So, the limits for death feigning beetles seem to lie somewhere around 50 percent relative humidity and below.

Death feigning beetle species live at low elevations where it is xeric (low humidity). This happens even though there is a large land mass with high average temperatures.

This explains their geographical distribution. It shows why these insects do not live in eastern Texas, Florida, or the Yucatan peninsula.

## Habitat

The fifteen death feigning beetle species live in the southwestern United States and north of the Isthmus of Tehuantepec in Mexico. Most species live in the Mojave, Sonoran, and Chihuahua deserts. There are some minimal expansions into Great Basin Desert habitats. The two exceptions to this are *Asbolus mexicanus* and *Cryptoglossa infausta*, which have ranges further east and north into Texas.

The habitats where death feigning beetles live include sand dunes, desert scrub, rocky crags and caves or lava tubes. Desert scrub is also known as xeric shrubland. Some cave-loving species will also use animal burrows.

The text presents some images of death feigning beetle habitats in the next few pages. Many species overlap in the same habitat. The image captions highlight species from a given habitat, but it is not a complete list. Chapter five covers individual species' distributions and habitats in more detail. You can also use Google Street View to take a virtual look around the areas where death feigning beetles live. Whether you are looking in the USA or Mexico, the habitats are very similar.

**Figure 3.13**
The Kelso Dunes area in California has multiple habitats in close proximity. Five species of Cryptoglossini can be found in this region of the Mojave Desert. *Asbolus verrucosus, Asbolus papillosus,* and *Cryptoglossa muricata* have all been found in the dunes area. The Dunes are pictured here.

**Figure 3.14**
Looking east from the Kelso Dunes there are mountains with lava tubes and caves. *Schizillus nunenmacheri* has been seen at the caves and lava tubes.

**Figure 3.15**
Looking south from the Kelso Dunes there are mountains with rocky slopes. *Schizillus laticeps* has been found there while *Cryptoglossa muricata* is more abundant in the low lying scrub area.

**Figure 3.16**
Desert scrub has vegetation that is usually less than 3-4 feet (1 meter) tall.

**Figure 3.17**
Cholla Gardens are in the foreground. Behind that are the mountains at the transition between the Mojave and Sonoran deserts. *Schizillus laticeps* has been found in the mountain region. Behind the mountains is the Imperial Valley where *Asbolus laevis* is frequently found in the dunes.

**Figure 3.18**
The Sonoran Desert north of Phoenix, Arizona, USA. Both *Cryptoglossa variolosa* and *Cryptoglossa muricata* can be found there.

**Figure 3.19**

The Grand Canyon rim is a high elevation region with no Cryptoglossini. However, *Cryptoglossa muricata* has been found down inside the canyon.

**Figure 3.20**

The northern edge of the range for Cryptoglossini in Texas, USA is near the city of Lubbock. It has semi-arid rolling plains with rocky grasslands and scrub. *Asbolus mexicanus* and *Cryptoglossa infausta* may inhabit this area.

**Figure 3.21**

The northeastern edge of the range for Cryptoglossini is near Austin, TX, USA. It includes the Pedernales riverbed and similar rocky waterways. These areas resemble the Chihuahua Desert in appearances. However, this is a savannah interspersed with oak and pine. It is a true east-meets-west region where yucca and prickly pear are also present. *Cryptoglossa infausta* is the only species that has been found this far northeast.

Going from the larger overview of the habitats, we can now look more closely at how those habitats differ. The desert areas differ in many ways. One is that the Mojave gets only one major rainy season per year. The rainy season is in the winter months. The Sonoran Desert gets two rainy seasons per year. One in winter and one in summer. Many consider the Baja California region to be a subregion of the Sonoran Desert. The Chihuahua desert gets rain in the summer into fall.

The plants that live in those regions are characteristic of each place. Joshua trees are abundant in the Mojave Desert. Saguaro cacti are the key indicator of Sonoran Desert. The Chihuahua desert lacks both species but has other yucca and many more cactus species.

We can also look closer at the terrain. We want to see how a rocky hillside, a sand dune, and a lava tube look up close. While we are at it, it might be good to examine the soil in different regions to see what it looks like too.

**Figure 3.22**
The Mojave and Sonoran deserts cover multiple states and many species of death feigning beetles live there. Joshua trees (left) are a type of yucca plant. They are more characteristic of the Mojave Desert. Saguaro cacti (right) are more characteristic of the Sonoran Desert.

**Figure 3.23**
A rocky canyon in the Sonoran desert. Loose gravel, plant material and sandy soil is built up in the valley.

**Figure 3.24**
Sand dunes (left) are favored by multiple species, while lava tubes (right) are known to be used by only *Schizillus nunenmacheri*. The floor of the tube is a dusty clay-like soil.

**Figure 3.25**

Sandy soil is the habitat for larvae. Sandy material was examined from the Sonoran Desert in the wash of a canyon (top left) west of Phoenix, Arizona, USA. Rocky sand beneath the scrub near Kelso, California, USA is in the top right. Kelso Dunes sand is in the bottom left. Larger grained sand from Twentynine Palms, California, USA is in the bottom right.

## Adaptations to the environment

Now we know where death feigning beetles are likely to live and the appearance of those habitats. But what do they do to survive? They can survive on a wide variety of plant and animal materials as food. Their ecological role is primarily as nutrient recyclers - like what earthworms do for moist environments. But, other than being omnivores, what makes them specifically adapted to a desert environment?

The blue death feigning beetle has many of the adaptations that we expect in the harsh desert environment. We can start with the blue color that is the result of a waxy coating. Some scientists think that the light reflecting off the waxy coating reduces the heat that otherwise would be generated if the beetle was mostly black. Wax is a normal feature of the exoskeleton's surface. Wax prevents desiccation (drying out) in nearly all insects. If left untouched in a dry environment, most death feigning beetles will show some accumulation of wax. The blue death feigning beetle has just taken it to an extreme.

**Figure 3.26**
Light shines through the elytra in this backlit teneral adult blue death feigning beetle. This reveals the sub-elytral cavity.

In all tenebrionids there is an empty space underneath the elytra. We call this space the **"subelytral cavity"**. This space offers several unique advantages to the beetles. The first is related to water loss. Tenebrionid beetles breathe through small holes in the sides of the thorax and abdomen called spiracles. There is a pair of exposed spiracles in the thorax. "Exposed" means they open to the air, but they hide in the space between the prothorax and the mesothorax. All other spiracles open into the subelytral cavity.

Breathing in does not cause water loss. Breathing out causes water loss. Some beetles can regulate the direction of air flow. They breathe in through the exposed thoracic spiracles. They breathe out through the others in the subelytral cavity. Beetles are able to trap humid air in the subelytral cavity. This might reduce water loss from the abdominal spiracles. The spiracles on some species are relatively small compared to others. This further reduces air exchange and water loss.

**Figure 3.27**
Enlarged forelegs are a hallmark of a subterranean larva.

A second advantage that the subelytral cavity offers is a space for the abdomen to expand. This expansion area allows beetles to load up on food and water in times of abundance so that they can go for long periods in times of famine and drought. The subelytral cavity is well-developed among death feigning beetles. While precise measurements of volume have not been made, *Asbolus verrucosus* seems to have the largest subelytral cavity while *Cryptoglossa variolosa* may have the smallest.

The legs of death feigning beetles and larvae also represent adaptations. Larvae of tenebrionids have adapted themselves for subterranean life. Their front legs are larger and have hardened tips that make them better for digging.

The legs of adult beetles also have advantages. The main advantages are that they are long and possess tarsal hairs. The long legs are proposed to allow the beetles to adjust their height above the hot sand, staying further away when they are too hot. They can rest on the surface to gain heat when they are too cool.

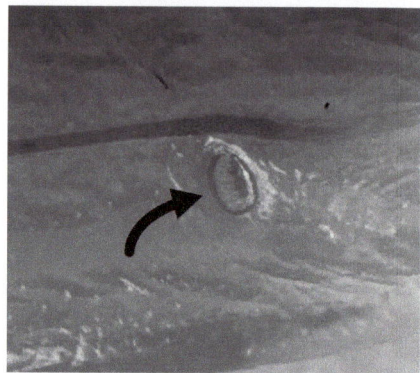

**Figure 3.28**

The top image shows obvious spiracles on the hickory horned devil. The bottom shows a spiracle on a mealworm. Spriacles are indicated by arrows.

The tarsal hairs act like brushes and allow individuals to sweep sand away. You might notice *Asbolus laevis* tends to dig quite a bit compared to other species if you keep them as pets. The long tarsal hairs help with this digging. The brushes also allow for traction when flipping themselves over.

Behavioral adaptations also exist. Darkling beetles hide from daylight. Death feigning beetles tend to be active at dusk and dawn. They are active in the nighttime. They have peak activities in spring and fall. No doubt this keeps them out of the hot desert sun most of the time. Some beetles live in caves and rodent dens to avoid the harsh desert environment. We can consider this to be a successful adaptation in behavior. Hiding is also a way of avoiding predators, given they have no defensive glands!

You might wonder what death feigning could do to help these beetles survive. Death feigning beetles and their larvae might be food for other organisms. Death feigning seems like a strategy to avoid looking good to eat. Not moving might evade some predators that require movement to feel vibrations of their prey (tarantulas). Some predators require movement to visually track and attack their prey (lizards). Lack of movement can thwart those kinds of predators.

**Figure 3.29**

The top image shows death feigning in an adult. The bottom shows death feigning in two larvae (left and center). The left-most larva is covered in debris due to blood adhering to its surface.

For the remaining predators, they might not need prey that moves once they have identified something worth eating. This is where long legs come in. You will see in Chapter 5 that many death feigning beetles play dead with their legs extended. By playing dead with the legs extended, it makes them bigger. They become too big to fit into the mouths of some predators. The only way for a predator with limited gape (mouth opening) to get a beetle into their mouth is to grab the beetle sideways or legs first. Death feigning makes the beetle difficult to eat because a legs-first meal is hard to swallow.

It is not surprising that many death feigning beetles also have pointy back ends. Imagine a predator trying to avoid the legs and swallow a beetle from the backside. What they get is a series of

**Figure 3.30**
A desert stink beetle showing headstanding behavior.

spikes in their mouth and throat. Thus, death feigning behavior in adults is beneficial on multiple levels when it is combined with structural features like long legs and spikes on the elytra.

Larvae of some death feigning beetle species will also feign death. In the blue death feigning beetle, the larvae sometimes reflex bleed. The lizards known to eat beetle larvae will only spend one or two seconds looking for food after digging in the sand. The reason these lizards are so impatient is that they have predators out to get them too! So, if a beetle larva can hide for more than a couple of seconds, then they probably have a good chance of surviving. In the case of blue death feigning beetle larvae, the average death feigning time is about 18 seconds. For the ones that bleed, they also get camouflaged with sand that sticks to the blood. This bloody fake death is, no doubt, an effective way to hide.

Head standing behavior also is common among death feigning beetles. Except for the blue death feigning beetle, headstanding is probably more common. Death feigning beetles do this to mimic stink beetles. In the same areas where death feigning beetles live, there are desert stink beetles that head stand. However, unlike death feigning beetles, these guys can produce some nasty smelling and tasting chemicals called quinones. Therefore, would-be predators learn not to mess with beetles that are head standing. By mimicking the desert stink beetles, death feigning beetles are also benefiting from head standing behavior.

For some species, larvae might undergo supernumerary molts. This allows them to avoid pupating during crowded conditions when they would be vulnerable to cannibalism.

Finally, there are genetic adaptations which we are just learning about. The blue death feigning beetle has extra copies of genes for resistance to heat stress, immune responses, and getting rid of toxic chemicals.

As you can see, there are many adaptations to protect death feigning beetles from the environment and predators.

### Section Summary

- Characteristics of the suborder Polyphaga are:
  - the hind coxa (metacoxa) does not pass beyond the first abdominal segment
  - they are missing notopleural sutures
- Characteristics of the family Tenebrionidae are:
  - they hide from daylight
  - 11 segmented antennae
  - 5-5-4 tarsal formula
  - notched eyes
  - subelytral cavity
- Characteristics of the Chryptoglossini
  - no stink glands!
  - large eggs
  - long-legged adults
  - larvae with large front legs
  - exarate pupae
  - play dead
  - head stand
  - live in the hot desert areas of the USA and Mexico
- Habitats differ in
  - location
  - elevation
  - rainfall
  - plant life
  - soil

# 4. DEATH FEIGNING BEETLE SPECIES

## 4.1 Key characteristics

### Genus level characteristics

As described earlier, you can divide the Cryptoglossini into three groups called **genera** (singular = genus). The name given to a genus is also known as a **generic name**. The **genus *Schizillus*** is easy to identify. A bump on each side of the head divides each eye into two parts. We call this bump the **"epistomal canthus"**. The epistomal canthus makes the beetle look as if it has four separate compound eyes. When viewed from the top, the eyes do not appear to reach the edge of the head. When viewed from the side, a very thin line connects the top half of the eye to the bottom half. There are no ommatidia in the connecting region. The name "*Schizillus*" contains the ancient Greek prefix *schizo-* which means "split" or "divided". It also contains the Latin suffix *-illus* which means "a small version". "*Schizillus*" means "small split". There are only two species in the genus *Schizillus*.

The **genus *Asbolus*** is closely related to *Schizillus*. Their eyes are not completely divided by an epistomal canthus on the side of the head. The eyes narrow greatly and wrap down around the lateral edge of the head. At the narrowest part, the region connecting the top and bottom portions of the eyes is only 3 ommatidia wide. The genus name is from a Greek word meaning "sooty". This likely is a reference to the surface wax. There are four species in the genus *Asbolus*.

The remaining death feigning beetles are in the **genus *Cryptoglossa***. The members of *Cryptoglossa* do not have narrowed or split eyes like the other two genera. The epistomal canthus is much smaller. At the narrowest region of the eyes, there are at least 5 ommatidia. There are nine species in the genus. The genus name, like the tribe name, means "hidden tongue".

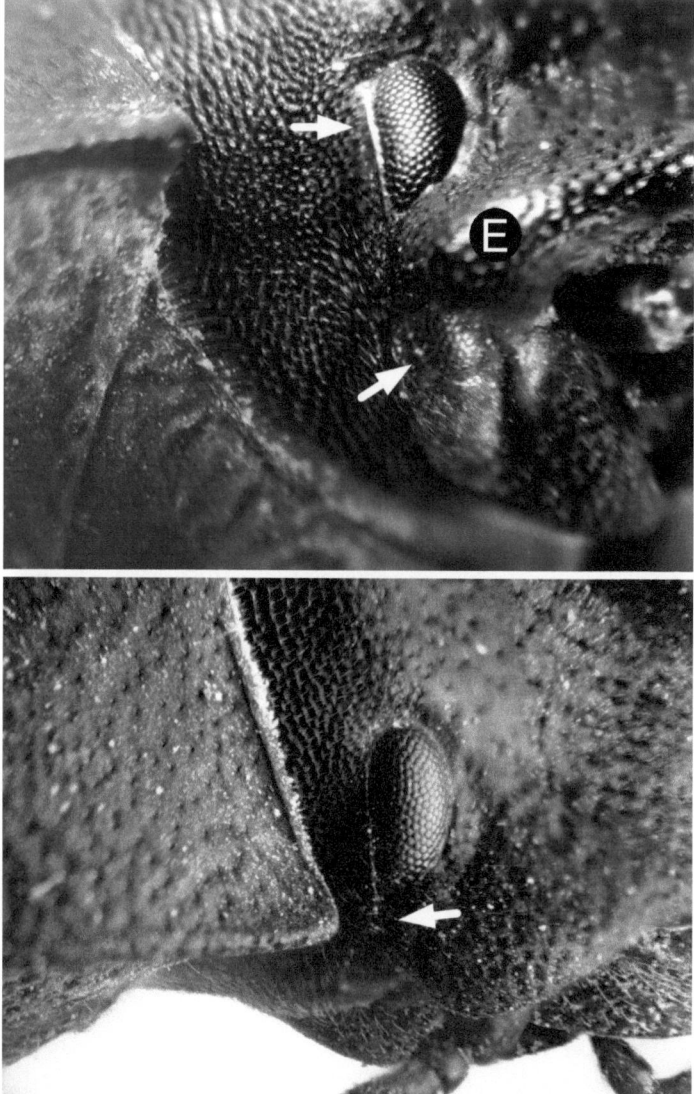

**Figure 4.1.1**
Side view of the eye of *Schizillus laticeps* (top) showing two separate eye regions indicated by white arrows. The epistomal canthus of the head is labeled with an "E" and divides the eye into two sections. A dorsal view (bottom) shows the top eye does not have ommatidia that wrap around the edge of the head (arrow). Anterior is to the right. Specimen courtesy of Peter Clausen.

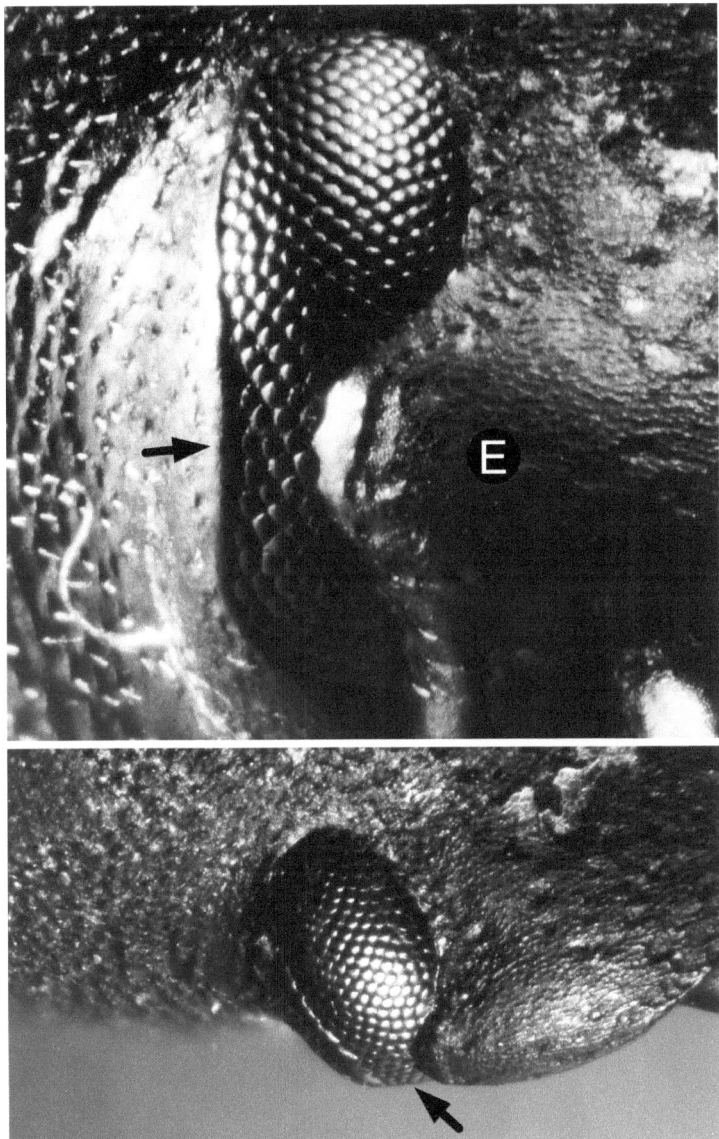

**Figure 4.1.2**
Side view of the eye of *Asbolus verrucosus* (top image). The narrow portion indicated by the black arrow has about four rows that are only three ommatidia wide. The epistomal canthus of the head is labeled with an "E". A dorsal view (bottom) shows the eye wraps around the edge and is not interrupted (arrow). Anterior is to the right.

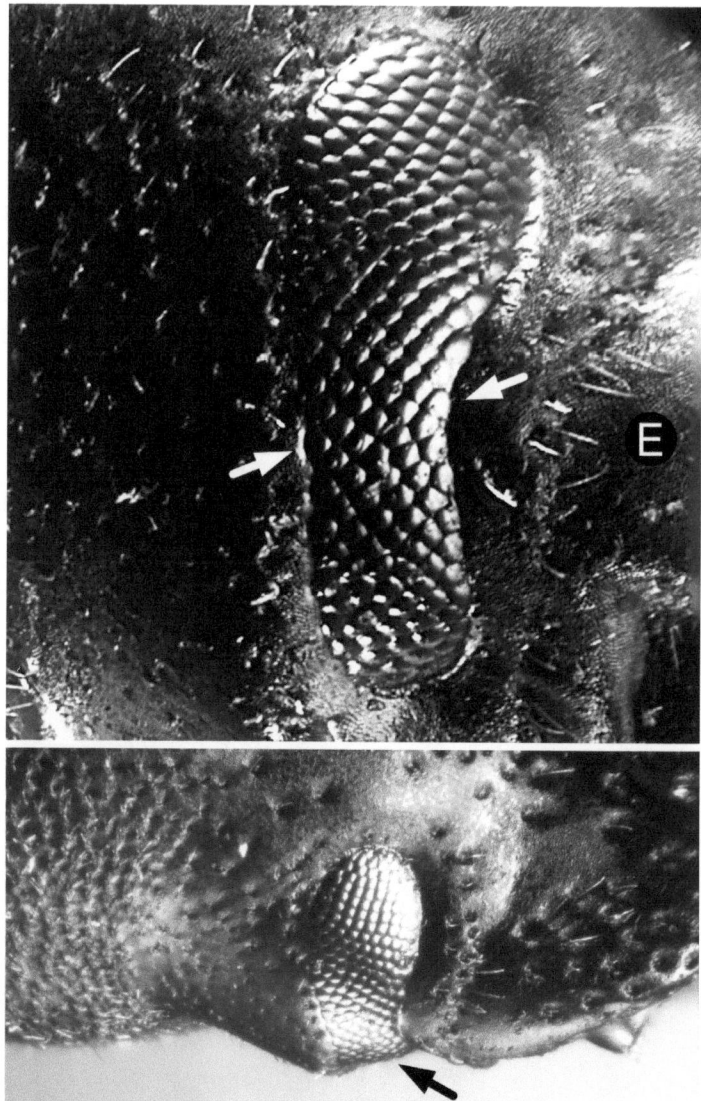

**Figure 4.1.3**
Side view of the eye of *Cryptoglossa muricata* (top image). The eye is roughly bean-shaped and is not substantially narrowed or divided by a lateral process. The white arrows show slanted rows that are five ommatidia wide. The epistomal canthus of the head is labeled with an "E". A dorsal view (bottom) shows the eye wraps around the edge (arrow) and is not interrupted. Anterior is to the right.

You might notice that the genus name is in italics. This is an international standard for zoological nomenclature. For all taxonomic categories at the genus level and below, we write these names in italics. The genus names will have a capital letter at the beginning. At the species level, the name includes the generic name and a second name called the **"species epithet"**. An example is *"Schizillus laticeps"*. We do not capitalize the species epithet. We can abbreviate the generic names using a single initial and a period when they are used to describe a species within the genus. *"S. laticeps"* is an example. By convention, we don't abbreviate this until after the generic name has been used at least once in a text. Thereafter, it is often abbreviated to save space.

**Figure 4.1.4**
This bee pronotum shows a central glabrous region surrounded by a pubescent margin containing many setae.

### Species level characteristics

The previous sections focused more on the anatomical parts of the insects, but morphology also includes surface features. The surface features and texture of the beetles is important. We want to understand these surface characteristics, so we can identify each death feigning beetle species. The pronotum of each species has

**Figure 4.1.5**
Flattened tubercles on the elytra of *Cryptoglossa variolosa* (left) and muricate tubercles/spicules on the elytra of *Cryptoglossa muricata* (right).

distinct characteristics. One characteristics is how rounded it is. It may be slightly **convex**. It may appear more rounded, as if inflated like a balloon. This inflated condition is referred to as **"globose"** in reference to a globe or sphere.

Some beetles have a smooth surface. Some beetles are hairy. We call an individual hair on an insect a **"seta"** (plural = setae). You can use **"pubescent"** to indicate the presence of setae. You can use **"glabrous"** to indicate the absence of setae.

Bumps of various sizes and shapes may cover the external surfaces. These bumps have special names too. The elytra have ten intervals or rows where these bumps may occur. The numbering of the **elytral intervals** begins at "1" near the elytral suture and ends at "10" on the **pseudoepipleural margin**. We call a large bump or protrusion a **"process"** - like the prosternal process on the thorax. A wart-like bump is referred to as a **"tubercle"**. A pimple-like, almost microscopic bump is referred to as a **"papilla"** (plural = papillae). The setae, tubercles and papillae may have more specialized appearances. Setae that are thicker and harder than a typical "hair" may be referred to as **"spicules"**. Oddly, we can also use the word spicule to describe a tubercle or larger papilla that is pointed or spiked. If tubercles are more pointy than wart-like, this condition may be referred to

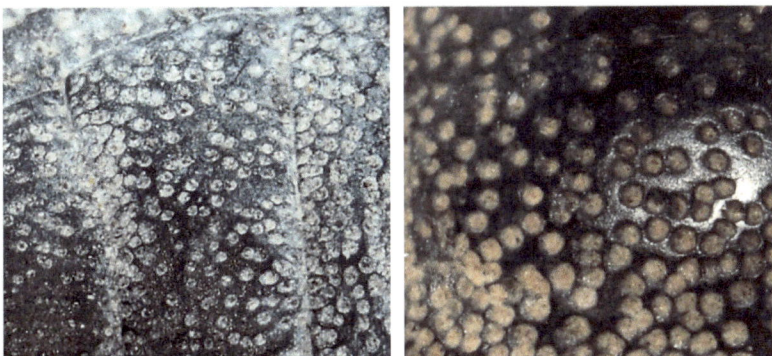

**Figure 4.1.6**
Punctate surfaces on the sternum of *Asbolus verrucosus* (left) and the pronotum of *Cryptoglossa variolosa* (right).

as **"muricate"**. In one death feigning beetle species, the tubercles fuse together to from long rib-like structures called **"costae"** (singular = costa). The word costa has multiple meanings in the insect and beetle worlds. Don't be surprised if you see it used differently elsewhere.

A relatively smooth surface may appear as if it has been punctured dozens of times by push pins. Such a hole-covered surface is referred to as **"punctate"**. Like the pubescent/glabrous story, when most specimens are punctate, and the oddball bug is lacking the numerous tiny holes, the surface is called **"impunctate"**.

Surfaces also may have grooves in them. Sometimes the grooves are very fine and deep like they were made with a knife. Other times they are shallow like someone lightly karate chopped some cookie dough. In both cases, the groove is called a **"sulcus"**. A sulcus differs from a suture. A suture occurs where two different parts meet. These surface modifications define the textures of death feigning beetles and are used to assist identification purposes.

### Section Summary
- Eye characteristics separate the genera
    - split into top and bottom = *Schizillus*
    - narrowed to 3 ommatidia = *Asbolus*
    - narrowed to 5 ommatidia = *Cryptoglossa*
- Pronotum may be
    - convex, globose or sculptured
    - with or without deep puncta
- Elytra may or may not possess
    - tubercles, spicules, papillae, costae
- Feet are pubescent with
    - long or short setae
- Antennae may have
    - longer or shorter antennomeres

## 4.2 Species descriptions

The remainder of this section will cover each death feigning beetle species. The text groups the species in alphabetical order by genus. The sections that follow describe what to expect and how to use the information presented for each species.

### Captive breeding data

Captive breeding is one of the most exciting parts of owning pet beetles. Knowing whether or not others have been successful can be helpful. Captive breeding successes are likely to change rapidly. Each section indicates the current status of breeding successes using a small box before the pronunciation guide.

*Key to the breeding successes*

### Pronunciation respelling

It can be embarrassing to mispronounce a new word... like when the wait staff in a fancy restaurant corrects you after you placed your order. But in the world of scientific names, few people will be capable of correcting you. Those that do, are also probably wrong anyway. One approach is to forgive yourself and others.

Taxonomists try to create species names from Latin words. Many scientific names are a mishmash of words from other languages. Taxonomists converted them into Latin-like written forms (including people's names). Classically-trained Latin scholars are quick to tell you these Latinized words are not actually Latin. These constructs are not a spoken language. So, the rules for Latin pronunciation are almost inconsequential.

Sometimes a small community of people uses a species name quite frequently. The people in that community can help guide you with what is the expected pronunciation. A few death feigning beetle species' names have actually been said out loud by taxonomists and other beetle enthusiasts! That has helped immensely with creating this guide.

The pronunciation guide presented here is about as unofficial as one can get. The goal here is to make things easy. A person familiar with American English should be able to sound out the word and say it with reasonable confidence.

There are a couple of challenges: the sounds of the letter "a" and "u" can behave differently. "UH" is used to represent the "a" sound found in the word "sofa". "AH" is used to represent the "a" sound found in "father". "AY" represents the "a" as in "ape". "OO" is used to represent the sound of "u" as in "blue". This is a pronunciation respelling. Whether or not the resulting sounds are the way the original taxonomist meant the words to sound remains unknown. Maybe we aren't supposed to say them out loud! They are certain to be Americanized and unlike anything a Latin scholar would advise.

So, do your best, and however you decide to pronounce a scientific name, do so with confidence. If you speak any scientific name out loud in a conversation and someone chooses to correct you... you must decide if you respect their opinion enough to change, or to keep doing it your way!

## Distribution map

Pink color highlights each state where a particular species has been found. Blue is used to show the rough locations of individual sightings. Whenever clusters of observations were reasonably close together, the cloud was extended. This was to fuse those observations into a larger contiguous region. In some species, their habitat is known to be dispersed. This is true for the cave-dwelling species or when two subspecies are separated by large distances. For those species, the distribution maps will contain several distinct locations. Location maps can help to determine which species you have discovered if the external morphology is ambiguous.

### Original discovery

The person that discovers a species often gets to name that species. This is not always true. Sometimes the person who originally collected a new species has other interests. It can sometimes be another person who identifies it as a novel species. These records reflect the history of a species and this section presents that brief history here. Additionally, new discoveries can cause revisions. The text provides some of that history here. The current taxonomy of the death feigning beetles is the result of detailed revision work done by the taxonomist Rolf L. Aalbu in the mid 1980s. Among other things, he discovered that *Asbolus papillosus* is a distinct species and not a subspecies of *Asbolus laevis*.

### Meaning of the scientific name

The etymology or the origin and meaning of the scientific name is presented here. Usually, this is a reflection of the physical appearance in some way. However, other meanings may exist, such as the location where the specimen was discovered or, in some cases, it is named in honor of a person. Care was taken to make sure the surname pronunciations follow what their descendants use.

### Unique features of the species

The text provides important features of a given species. It also gives additional information on how they differ from other species that might cause confusion.

### Photographs

Some excellent nature photographers provided photographs of living specimens for the majority of species. The section provides images that highlight the unique features of a species whenever possible.

## 4.2.1 *Asbolus laevis*
C  ASS-BOWL-US LEE-VISS

*Asbolus laevis* was originally described by John Lawrence LeConte

in 1851. In Latin, "*laevis*" means smooth (or at least lacking in hairs or roughness). *A. laevis* is one of the two species whose geographical distribution is limited to sand dunes running north to south near the border of California and Arizona into northwestern Mexico. It tends to be found on the leeward side of the dunes where sand is more finely grained. The pronotum of *A. laevis*, like that of *A. papillosus*, is globose, and lacks sulci. *A. laevis* can be distinguished from

*Asbolus laevis* (captive raised) photo by S. Dean Rider Jr.

other *Asbolus* species by its more smooth shiny elytra and long setae on the tarsi. Tarsal setae are greater than 1.5 times the length of the tarsomeres. Papillae on the elytra, if present, are restricted to the lateral edges. Internally, the female reproductive tract bears an ovipositor that is two thirds the length and notably wider in comparison to that of *A. papillosus*. These are very active beetles in captivity, and they spend a great amount of time digging in the sand. They are often offered for sale as smooth death feigning beetles.

## 4.2.2 *Asbolus mexicanus*
C  ASS-BOWL-US MEX-E-CAN-NUSS

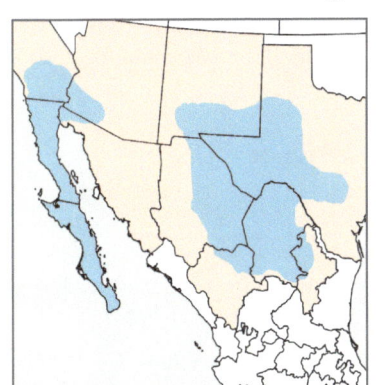

*Asbolus mexicanus* was originally described by George Charles Champion in 1884. This has a Latinized form of the Spanish word meaning "from Mexico". There are two subspecies separated geographically by the Sierra Madre Occidental pine-oak forest range. The pronotum of *A. mexicanus* is less inflated than the other *Asbolus* species, and is broadly convex. The elytra are variable in surface, depending on the subspecies. The tarsi do not have elongated setae. The eastern subspecies is referred to as *A. mexicanus mexicanus*. It has more smooth elytra. This species tends to be associated with limestone caves throughout its eastern range. The western subspecies is referred to as *A. mexicanus angularis*. It has a more rough surface on the elytra.

*Asbolus mexicanus mexicanus* (captive raised) photo by S. Dean Rider Jr. (Specimen courtesy of Tristan Shanahan).

## 4.2.3 *Asbolus papillosus*

 ASS-BOWL-US PAP-PILL-OH-SUSS

*Asbolus papillosus* was originally described by Charles Albert Triplehorn in 1964 as a subspecies of *Asbolus laevis*. It was moved to the species level by Rolf Aalbu (ca 1985) because internal features suggest it is a separate species. "*Papillosus*" is Latin for having papillae. *A. papillosus* is almost exclusively found around sand dunes and is far rarer than *A. laevis* in the areas where both species overlap (1 in

100 specimens). Externally, it is unique from *A. laevis* because of the numerous papillae on the elytra which dulls the surface and the short setae on the tarsomeres.

*Asbolus papillosus* photo by Hartmut Wisch.

*Asbolus papillosus* mesotarsus on the left (photo by Hartmut Wisch) compared to *Asbolus laevis* mesotarsus on the right (photo by S. Dean Rider Jr.). Note the relative length of setae in the two species.

## 4.2.4 *Asbolus verrucosus*

C   ASS-BOWL-US VAIR-ROO-COSE-US

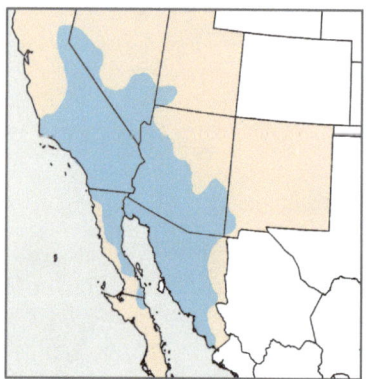

*Asbolus verrucosus* was originally described by John Lawrence LeConte in 1851. "*Verrucosus*" is Latin for "warty". *A. verrucosus* is widely distributed in sand flats and alkali scrub. It is the dominant animal in the northern Mojave desert where its biomass is greater than any other animal group examined (birds, lizards, mammals and snakes). *A. verrucosus* is unique in that the pronotum is both inflated and sculpted by three sulci to generate a four-lobed appearance. It is common in the pet trade as the blue death feigning beetle. The intensity of the wax-based blue color is humidity dependent and most prominent in dry conditions. It is sometimes called the desert ironclad beetle although it is not an ironclad beetle. Ironclad beetles are in the family Zopheridae.

*Asbolus verrucosus* photo by S. Dean Rider Jr.

## 4.2.5 *Cryptoglossa asperata*

X  CRIP-TOE-GLOSS-UH ASS-PUR-RAH-TUH

*Cryptoglossa asperata* was originally described by George Henry Horn in 1870. *"Asperata"* is the feminine version of the Latin word *"asperatus"*, which means rough or uneven - roughened. *C. asperata* appears to be restricted to Baja California Sur. Populations are present on some of the islands near the west coast of the Gulf of California. *C. asperata* has a smooth convex pronotum with no lobes but the elytra resemble those of *Asbolus verrucosus*. The elytra are rough with tubercles present. It differs from both *C. infausta* and *C. variolosa* by lacking the densely punctate head or

*Cryptoglossa asperata* photo by Steven Mlodinow.

pronotum. Three subspecies exist. *C. asperata discreta* is island located (Carmen, Espiritu Santo, Gallina, San Diego, San Francisco, San Jose, Partida) and has widely separated (discrete) tubercles on the elytra compared to the other two subspecies whose tubercles are more flattened and coalesced. *C. asperata subornata* is also present on the islands in the Gulf of California (Carmen, Cerralvo, Monserate, Pardo, and Santa Catalina). Its tubercles are highly reduced. *C. asperata asperata* is present on the peninsula and also some islands (Blanco, Coronados, Coyote, Danzante and Ildefonso).

## *4.2.6 Cryptoglossa bicostata*

X CRIP-TOE-GLOSS-UH BYE-COAST-AH-TUH

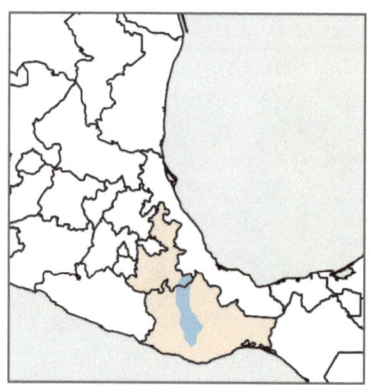

*Cryptoglossa bicostata* was originally described by Antoine Joseph Jean Solier in 1836. "Bicostata" is a Latinized word derived from "*bi*" for two and "*costa*" for ribs, so the meaning is "two-ribbed". This is a rarely encountered species that seems to be restricted to dry valleys in the states of Oaxaca and Puebla, Mexico. Recent sightings were concentrated in the Loma El Toro region in the state of Puebla off highway 125. Other recent sightings include one a few kilometers southeast of San Rafael, Puebla, MX, and outside of Guadalupe de los Obos in Oaxaca, MX. *C. bicostata* is easily identified by the fused tubercles that form costae on each elytron. The costae are formed on elytral intervals 2 and 5. The costa on interval 2 is much shorter than the costa on interval 5, which runs almost the entire length of the elytron.

*Cryptoglossa bicostata* photo by Barry Sullender.

## 4.2.7 Cryptoglossa caraboides

 CRIP-TOE-GLOSS-UH CARE-AB-OH-EYE-DEEZ

*Cryptoglossa caraboides* was originally described by Count Carl Gustaf Mannerheim in 1843. The original description (translated) indicated that it possesses triple posterior spines. As Mannerheim was a beetle taxonomist it seems unlikely the name it was given was a reference to the family of ground beetles (Carabici during their time), in which he did extensive work. The suffix *-oides* is a Latinized version of the Greek *"ides"* meaning "looks like". *"Carabus"* (Latin) has multiple meanings, but in this context could mean crab as opposed to a specific type of boat. Thus, *"caraboides"* might mean "crab-like". *C. caraboides* is restricted to central Mexico

and does not overlap in geographic range with the morphologically similar *C. michelbacheri*. *C. caraboides* is distinguished morphologically from *C. michelbacheri* by having a smooth, impunctate concave region in the middle of the metafemur. Only *Schizillus nunenmacheri* has a similar impunctate region on its lateral metafemur. The larger spikes on the elytra of *C. caraboides* are restricted to intervals 8 and 10 near the pseudoepipleural margin, while in *C. michelbacheri* they are on interval 9. No images of live *C. caraboides* were available to be presented here.

## 4.2.8 *Cryptoglossa infausta*

C  CRIP-TOE-GLOSS-UH IN-FOW-STUH

*Cryptoglossa infausta* was originally described by John Lawrence LeConte in 1854. "Infaustus" means unlucky in Latin; "*infausta*"

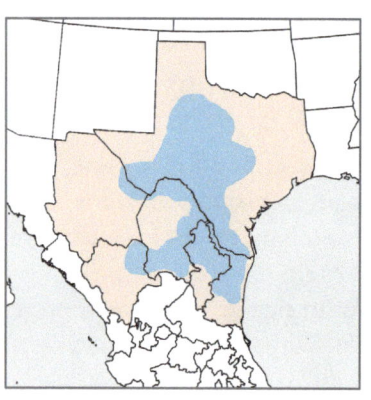

being the feminine form. This species is restricted to the Chihuahua desert and central Texas where it is sometimes found under prickly pear, under rocks and in caves. *C. infausta* is oval in appearance, with a deeply punctate head and flattened tubercles on the elytra. It lacks the densely punctate surface on the pronotum like that found in *C. variolosa*. This species is encountered somewhat frequently and is sometimes offered in the pet trade.

*Cryptoglossa infausta* photo by S. Dean Rider Jr.

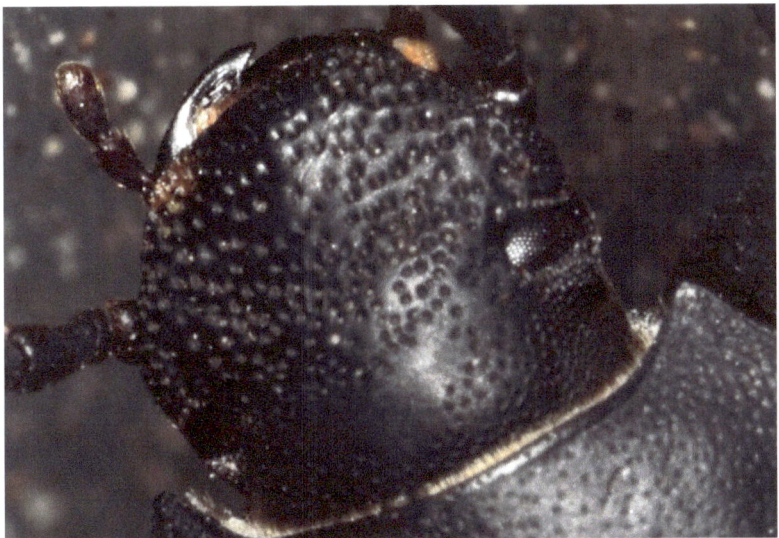
*Cryptoglossa infausta* photo by S. Dean Rider Jr. Note the deeply punctate head and small shallow puncta on the pronotum.

## 4.2.9 *Cryptoglossa michelbacheri*

[X] CRIP-TOE-GLOSS-UH MICK-EL-BOCK-ER-EYE

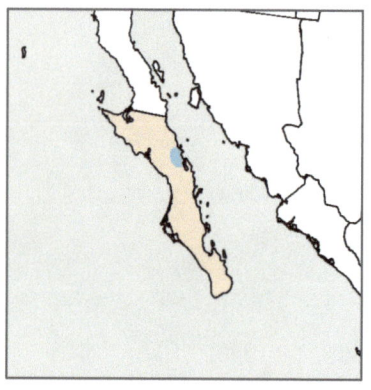

*Cryptoglossa michelbacheri* was originally described by Frank Ellsworth Blaisdell in 1943. A Latinized form for a surname used as species epithet is called a patronym. The name "michelbacheri" is a patronym based on the surname of Abe Ezra Michelbacher. Along with Edward Shearman Ross, he collected the original type series on an expedition to lower California's peninsula in 1938. The expedition was needed to replace some large museum collections (originally from 1888 and 1894) that were destroyed by earthquakes and fire. *C. michelbacheri* is restricted to Baja California Sur and does not overlap in range to the morphologically similar *C. caraboides*. *C. michelbacheri* is distinguishable from *C. caraboides* by geographic location and morphologically by having a punctate surface in the middle of the metafemur. *C. michelbacheri* has only been collected in Baja California Sur in the region along federal highway 1 between Santa Rosalia and El Coyote on the north end of Concepcion Bay. There are no images presented here for *C. michelbacheri*.

## 4.2.10 *Cryptoglossa muricata*

[C] CRIP-TOE-GLOSS-UH MUR-ICK-CAW-TUH

*Cryptoglossa muricata* was originally described by John Lawrence LeConte in 1851. "*Muricata*" is the feminine Latin form of "*muricatus*" which means rough with short, hard points (studded).

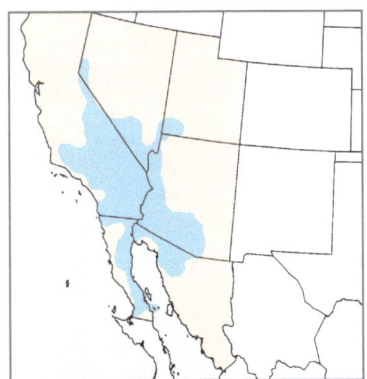

*C. muricata* is widely distributed and is associated with rocky hillsides and coarsely grained substrates. It is frequently found in the vicinity of plants (cholla, creosote bushes, Joshua trees, and yucca). Elytral surfaces are covered by pointed tubercles or spicules (muricate) that are not limited to one or two rows of spicules at the elytral margins. It is overall longer and more slender than other species. This species is commonly available in the pet trade as the studded or rough death feigning beetle.

*Cryptoglossa muricata* photo by S. Dean Rider Jr.

## 4.2.11 *Cryptoglossa seriata*

 CRIP-TOE-GLOSS-UH SAIR-REE-AH-TUH

*Cryptoglossa seriata* was originally described by John Lawrence LeConte in 1861. "*Seriata*" is derived from the feminine form for

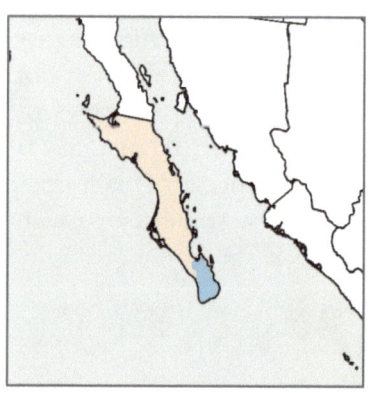

the Latin word "*seriatus*" which is "to be arranged in a series", or in rows (i.e. dotted lines on elytra). *C. seriata* is restricted to the southern tip of Baja California Sur (the cape region). Morphologically, this species is easily separated from the other *Cryptoglossa* species because the prosternal process is missing. There are two subspecies. *C. seriata seriata* is present on the peninsula and possesses evenly and serially punctate elytra. *C. seriata cerralvoensis* has centrally punctate elytra and is geographically restricted to Cerralvo Island.

*Cryptoglossa seriata* photo by Álvaro San José Elizundia.

## 4.2.12 *Cryptoglossa spiculifera*

 CRIP-TOE-GLOSS-UH SPIK-KUL-IFF-ERR-UH

*Cryptoglossa spiculifera* was originally described by John Lawrence LeConte in 1861. The Latin "*spiculum*" is derived from "*spicum*" (spike) as a diminutive version of a spike (a sharp needle like point). Adding the suffix "*ifera*", meaning bearing, creates the meaning of "covered in little spikes". *C. spiculifera* is found in quite a variety of microhabitats in southern California, Baja California and Baja California Sur. It has been found in caves, on beaches, in agricultural areas, thorn forests, dunes, scrub, and

*Cryptoglossa spiculifera* photo by Robin Gwen Agarwal.

the nests of wood rats and birds (osprey and pelican). *C. spiculifera* is distinguished from *C. muricata* by lacking spicules on the dorsal medial surfaces of the elytra. Spicules are restricted to the lateral edges of the elytra in 2-3 rows. The pronotum has surface sculpturing, but it is not as pronounced as that seen in *A. verrucosus*. The pronotum is less punctate than that of *C. muricata* and the prosternal process is reduced in size. This species has two subspecies that are difficult to distinguish because there are some intermediate forms. *C. spiculifera pectoralis* is in the northern part of the range (north of Loreto, Baja California Sur), has more parallel sides, and a densely punctate 4th abdominal sternite. *C. spiculifera spiculifera* is more rounded in shape, is restricted to the cape region of Baja California Sur (south of Loreto), and the 4th abdominal sternite is impunctate.

*Cryptoglossa spiculifera pectoralis* photo by Robin Gwen Agarwal. Note the last visible abdominal sternite is punctate.

## 4.2.13 *Cryptoglossa variolosa*
[L] CRIP-TOE-GLOSS-UH VAIR-REE-OH-LOW-SAH

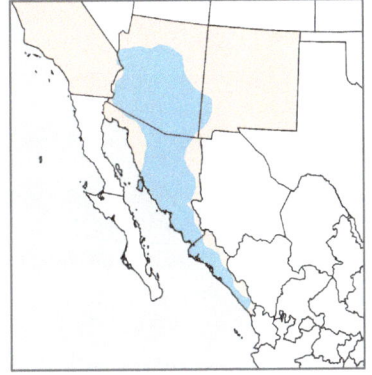

*Cryptoglossa variolosa* was originally described by George Henry Horn in 1870. The feminine version of the Latin word "*variolosus*" means smallpox (or variegated). In the Arizona upland, Sonoran plains and Sonoran foothills, *C. variolosa* is associated with areas where succulents are abundant. *C. variolosa* has a densely punctate head, punctate pronotum and underside as well as flattened tubercles on the elytra. It is sold as the black death feigning beetle but frequently is covered in a pinkish beige coating.

*Cryptoglossa variolosa* photo by S. Dean Rider Jr.

## 4.2.14 *Schizillus laticeps*
[L] SKIZ-ILL-US LAT-ISS-EPPS

*Schizillus laticeps* was originally described by George Henry Horn in 1874. *"Laticeps"* is derived from the Latin word *"latis"*, for broad. This is used in combination with the suffix *"-ceps"*, meaning "-headed", so *laticeps* means "broad-headed". *S. laticeps* is most abundant in the Mojave Desert where it is found in rocky canyons, sometimes at higher elevations (1200 meters; 3900 feet). It is sometimes found hiding under rocks, plants and debris. Unlike in *S. nunenmacheri*, the third segment of the antenna is shorter than the combined length of the next two segments. It also has punctate lateral surfaces on its metafemurs.

*Schizillus laticeps* photo by S. Dean Rider Jr. Specimen from Peter Clausen.

## 4.2.15 *Schizillus nunenmacheri*

 SKIZ-ILL-US NOON-ENN-MOCK-ER-EYE

*Schizillus nunenmacheri* was originally described by Frank Ellsworth Blaisdell in 1921. The name is a patronym to honor Frederick William Nunenmacher, a Coleopterist who focused on the family Coccinellidae. *S. nunenmacheri* is a cave-dwelling species that can sometimes be found in lava tubes and the burrows of packrats. The third segment of the antenna is longer than the combined length of the next two segments, but not quite as long as the combined length of the next three segments.

*Schizillus nunenmacheri* photo by Vahe Martirosyan.

### Section Summary

- Each species is unique in the following ways
  - morphology
  - geographical distribution
  - habitat preference
- Species reported only in the USA
  - *Asbolus papillosus*
  - *Schizillus nunenmacheri*
- Species reported only in Mexico
  - *Cryptoglossa asperata*
  - *Cryptoglossa bicostata*
  - *Cryptoglossa caraboides*
  - *Cryptoglossa michelbacheri*
  - *Cryptoglossa seriata*
- Species found in both countries
  - *Asbolus laevis*
  - *Asbolus mexicanus*
  - *Asbolus verrucosus*
  - *Cryptoglossa infausta*
  - *Cryptoglossa muricata*
  - *Cryptoglossa spiculifera*
  - *Cryptoglossa variolosa*
  - *Schizillus laticeps*

## 4.3 Cheat sheets

Dozens of robust characters can be used to compare death feigning beetle species. A small number are enough to serve as diagnostic markers. Remember that the characteristics of the beetle's eyes separate the different genera. You can then use the cheat sheets to minimize the time you need to identify these species. Simply look at the feature and follow the row to the filled circle. Then look at the column heading to see what species possesses that feature. Sometimes two or more species share a feature. There is at least one combination of characteristics that sets each species apart.

### Cheat sheet for *Schizillus* species

|  | *Schizillus laticeps* | *Schizillus nunenmacheri* |
|---|---|---|
| Length of antenna segment 3 < 4 + 5 | ● |  |
| Length of antenna segment 3 > 4 + 5 |  | ● |

### Cheat sheet for *Asbolus* species

|  | *Asbolus laevis* | *Asbolus mexicanus* | *Asbolus papillosus* | *Asbolus verrucosus* |
|---|---|---|---|---|
| Tarsal setae ~1.5x tarsomere length | ● |  |  |  |
| Pronotum not inflated |  | ● |  |  |
| Elytra with papillae |  |  | ● |  |
| Pronotum lobed |  |  |  | ● |

## Cheat sheet for *Cryptoglossa* species

| Feature | *Cryptoglossa bicostata* | *Cryptoglossa seriata* | *Cryptoglossa variolosa* | *Cryptoglossa infausta* | *Cryptoglossa asperata* | *Cryptoglossa caraboides* | *Cryptoglossa michelbacheri* | *Cryptoglossa muricata* | *Cryptoglossa spiculifera* |
|---|---|---|---|---|---|---|---|---|---|
| Elytra bearing costae | • | | | | | | | | |
| No prosternal process | | • | | | | | | | |
| Elytra covered in flattened tubercles | | | • | • | • | | | | |
| Densely punctate head | | | • | • | | | | | |
| Densely punctate pronotum | | | • | | | | | | |
| One row of spicules along elytral edge | | | | | | • | • | | |
| Mesal metafemur impunctate, concave | | | | | | • | | | |
| Elytra covered in sharp tubercles or spicules | | | | | | | | • | |
| Two rows of spicules along elytral edge | | | | | | | | | • |

## 5. THE BESTEST PETS

Death feigning beetles make great pets for beginners. They tolerate a wide range of temperatures. They accept a variety of foods. Young people can even hold them. These beetles are unable to climb smooth surfaces because they lack sticky pads on their tarsi. Death feigning beetles cannot fly because they possess fused outer elytra. Their flying wings are either non-functional or absent. In short, they are easy to care for.

Regulations on collecting and keeping pet insects vary widely, and will not be covered here. If you are lucky enough to live near where these beetles live, you can collect them yourself. If you live outside their range, you can purchase pet beetles. You can order them online if you don't find them in a local pet store. Either way, these beetles are great for both beginners and advanced beetle enthusiasts. More advanced individuals may want to try their hand at breeding these beetles. If your breeding is successful, you may choose to donate specimens to scientific research.

## Obtaining beetles

Not far in the past, there were only a few places you could buy a wild-caught death feigning beetle. Their popularity has soared in recent years. You can find them for sale from many vendors in the United States that sell invertebrates online. Usually, this is a side offering from an established reptile or tarantula dealer. They have even been sold in pet stores in the Midwestern states.

Some problems might arise. Not everyone knows which species they are selling. Not everyone uses the same common names. You might, for example, search for "black death feigning beetle for sale". One vendor might have *C. variolosa* for sale while another has *A. laevis* for sale. Similarly, if you are trying to locate a specimen of *S. laticeps* and the vendor actually has *C. muricata*, don't be shocked. You still can be disappointed. The four most abundant and readily available species are *A. verrucosus*, *C. variolosa*, *A. laevis*, and *C. muricata*. It seems likely that their discoverers would have referred to those beetles as warty, variegated, smooth, and muricate death feigning beetles (respectively). Would you rather call *A. verrucosus* a blue death feigning beetle or a warty death feigning beetle?

Each species has its own preferred habitats. The previous sections on each species provided geographical locations (when possible). Location and habitat information helps you find the beetles you want. Walking the desert may be most fruitful at dusk or dawn, as most species are crepuscular. Most species are active from about April through October. Summer months are the peak season for finding specimens. Many people have collected specimens while walking in the desert at night. Other people find specimens by turning over rocks and debris during daytime. It is advisable that if you flip over rocks in the desert, wear thick leather gloves. Also, lift rocks so that they open away from you in case something like a venomous snake happens to have claimed that space. Because these beetles like to hide when the sun is up,

**Figure 5.1**

Starting a pitfall trap. Choose a location for your trap such as near a bush (top) and collect your materials, including local rocks (bottom).

**Figure 5.2**
Finish your trap. Bury your container so the top is flush with the surrounding ground (top) and hide the trap with rocks from the surrounding region (bottom). Make sure the gap between the cover rock and the ground will allow beetles in.

overcast or cloudy days might be more likely to have beetles running about in the daytime. The activity of the beetles is also temperature dependent. Beetles reportedly are more active at temperatures above 50°F (10°C) or below 86°F (30°C).

Pitfall trapping is a good collection method. Trapping has been done to collect living specimens. If you would like to try trapping, a pitfall trap is pretty straight forward. The trap consists of a plastic party cup buried in the ground so that the top edge of the container is flush with the ground. You can use any smooth-walled container in place of a cup. Three small rocks or bits of wood that are a bit taller than a beetle are then placed around the container's perimeter. Place a flat rock that is larger than the container over the top so that it is resting on the three supports (rocks/wood). Ideal locations for such traps include: near rocks, under bushes, or near rodent burrows.

Some people report that molasses attracts death feigning beetles. Dead insects are also likely to be an effective bait. The beetles will make their way into the container, either because they are looking to hide, or because they are attracted to bait. Once inside, they are not able to climb the walls of the container and will remain trapped.

For living specimens, some shelter inside the trap may help. Checking the traps daily is the most important thing to do. You want to collect the specimens before something bad happens to them. For collecting dead specimens you can pour a little ethylene glycol (antifreeze) into the party cup when you make the trap. The antifreeze preserves the insects that fall in. The liquid will remain for months without evaporating.

## Housing

Creating a desert beetle tank for display in your living room, bedroom, office, or anywhere you want is exciting. The types of housing you can use is really as varied as you can imagine. A tank for pet beetles can be as barren or as elaborate as you desire. You can choose to set up a desert-like scene with sand, cholla wood, cork bark, rocks and cacti or maybe even a bleached skull. It is

**Figure 5.3**

*Asbolus verrucosus* is a very robust and popular pet. Here, beetles are being housed in a decorative enclosure made from a tequila bottle in a southwest themed display. Display and photograph by French J. Damewood IV.

important to make sure you provide places for the beetles to hide. Beetles do best in dry conditions. Ventilation is extremely important for desert beetles, so having a screened lid or an open top will be beneficial. If you have substrate, it might be good to use sand or gravel. You want to use something that can be compacted.

You can add plants. Artificial plants are much easier and probably safer to use for two reasons: they won't die, and they won't have pesticides on them. There is always a risk for pesticide residues to be present on ornamental plants.

If you use an aquarium with a metal lid, you have a lot of options for heating and lighting. If you plan to locate your beetles in a room that has lower temperatures, consider adding a heat lamp. Small heat lamps are available for small tanks. Ceramic bulbs tend to last a lot longer than the red incandescent bulbs. Do not try to substitute a chicken heat lamp for an insect or reptile lamp. Chicken lamps are far too strong for use with most aquarium setups. Heating bulbs work well with metal screen lids or with a setup that allows you to suspend the lamp over the tank.

**Figure 5.4**
A display beetle tank with a desert-like theme.

**Figure 5.5**
A practical setup of 2.5 gallon (9.4 liters) tanks for egg laying and collection. Metal lids, mini light domes on timers, 40 watt ceramic heat lamps, and conical bottom tubes plugged with cotton balls (used for water). Small pots are for hiding.

For small tanks or plastic tubs in cold rooms, a heating pad is a good choice in combination with LED lighting (if desired). You can place both lamps and lights on timers to help regulate temperature. This will also allow you to see your beetles during the hours you want. You can also use lights for aesthetic reasons.

As far as target temperatures go, having a spot in the tank that reaches around 80°F (26°C) is a reasonable goal.

A heat lamp of about 40 watts works well for small tanks around 2-5 gallons (7-18 liters) with metal lids. Lamps can be scaled up for larger tanks. A 24-hour timer outlet to switch the lamp on and off every other hour helped keep the temp around 80°F (26°C). Heat only during the daytime and turn the lamp off for 12 hours overnight. Surface temperatures can be measured with a no-contact thermometer.

Once you setup your housing, and you have added your beetles, these beetles will be amazing pets. They are very active and curious beetles. They will be active mostly at sunrise and sunset, which is when most people are at home. Therefore, their schedule will probably fit well with your schedule. One additional thing to consider is that you can keep these beetles communally with other beetle species, velvet ants and scorpions!

## Food and water

Tenebrionid beetles and many other insects have a dietary requirement for biotin. It is unlikely that your beetles will suffer from a biotin deficiency. Keep in mind that some foods like raw eggs may have a protein called avidin that prevents biotin from being available as a nutrient. Otherwise, biotin is an abundant vitamin and most raw foods contain at least trace amounts. There are no set rules on what you can try to feed your beetles. They are capable of surviving on a wide range of foods including fruits, vegetables, meat and dead insects. Perhaps one of the most interesting things about owning these beetles is offering them new foods to see how they behave. These beetles are adapted to desert conditions. You do not need to feed them in abundance all the time. In fact, they can go for relatively long periods of time without food or water. So, if you toss in some food before a vacation, you're probably good for a couple of weeks without any concerns. On the other hand, some beetle keepers prefer to add in only small amounts of food at a time. This is so that it is all consumed in a day or two. This approach helps to prevent

**Figure 5.6**
*Asbolus verrucosus* took no interest in a strawberry offered as food.

**Figure 5.7**
*Asbolus verrucosus* enjoying a carrot.

opportunistic mites and insects from becoming unwanted pests within your beetle tank.

If you provide foods that are moist, or frequently mist your tank, you may not need to provide additional water. But, if you do provide water, there are common ways to do so. One easy way is to have a shallow dish with a few pebbles in it for the beetles to crawl on. They have access to the water. The rocks keep them from possibly submerging or drowning. A second watering option

**Figure 5.8**
Bacon seems to draw a crowd.

**Figure 5.9**
Death feigning beetles enjoying a drink of water from a shallow dish with pebbles in it.

that lasts much longer is a pill bottle or test tube filled with water and plugged with cotton balls. The beetles can obtain water from the moist cotton end. The small surface area of the cotton plug prevents rapid evaporation of the water in the tube. This is a great choice for vacations or if you are kind of lazy (ahem, very busy with other things).

## Death Feigning behavior

As their common name suggests, death feigning beetles play dead. The fancy term for this is "thanatosis". Different species have slightly different behaviors. Some prefer to head stand. Others will play dead for hours. These variations can exist between individuals. The same individual may behave differently from one time to another.

It may seem like overkill to show seven different species of death feigning beetles playing dead, but this allows you to compare and contrast what they look like when they take on this behavior. One thing they have in common is that their pose almost always has the legs suspended in the air, never spread out and touching the ground. Legs on the ground means they are dead, not playing dead. Don't be fooled by their deception. A peculiar difference includes tarsal twitches in *Asbolus laevis*. Eighty percent of *Cryptoglossa muricata* will probably head stand after death feigning. If other interesting behaviors occur, the observations need to be shared. These might help distinguish different species from one another.

## Decorating beetles

It is common for biologists to tag individuals or mark them in some way so that they can be monitored for research purposes. Common reasons include being able to identify specific individuals or to estimate population size. This is true in entomology as well. We can adapt this strategy for a more entertaining purpose. We can decorate beetles with paint and jewels! However, we need to be aware of the biology of the beetle

**Figure 5.10**
*Asbolus laevis* playing dead.

**Figure 5.11**
*Asbolus mexicanus* playing dead.

**Figure 5.12**
*Asbolus verrucosus* playing dead.

**Figure 5.13**
*Cryptoglossa infausta* playing dead.

**Figure 5.14**
*Cryptoglossa variolosa* playing dead.

**Figure 5.15**
*Cryptoglossa muricata* playing dead.

**Figure 5.16**
*Cryptoglossa muricata* head standing.

**Figure 5.17**
*Schizillus laticeps* playing dead.

**Figure 5.18**
Beetles that are actually dead. Note how the legs and antennae are touching the ground. Top image is *Asbolus verrucosus* and bottom image is *Asbolus laevis*. If the beetles are recently deceased, their legs will be pliable and easily moved with a light touch, whereas beetles that are pretending will have rigidly held legs in the air.

**Figure 5.19**

Decorating Beetles. Cleaning with grain alcohol (top left) and painting with nail polish (top right). Bottom panels include painted beetle examples and one where gold leaf was glued to the elytra.

to avoid harming them. Therefore, any decorations are best done only on the dorsal/medial regions of the elytra and the pronotum. It is important not to seal off any body parts. This might shut off their access to air circulation. When done properly, these bejeweled beetles can thrive just as well as their untouched counterparts.

The process is simple. First, you need to remove the wax on the surfaces where you plan to paint or glue materials. You can use a cotton tipped applicator moistened in grain alcohol. Alcohol dissolves the waxy layer. A little rub with the wet tip and dry with the other tip gets rid of the wax. To make the alcohol dry faster, blow a little stream of air on the beetle for a few seconds to help. Once the beetle is dry, it is time for decorations. A fast-drying nail polish is a great marking agent. You can find them in just about any color... with or without sparkles. It is up to your imagination and skill to make a beetle that is aesthetically pleasing. If you plan to add other things like gold leaf, artificial nails, or small crystals, high strength waterproof PVA wood glue works well as an adhesive. You can use a toothpick to apply very small amounts of glue. Now you really can have any color beetle you want!

### Longevity

Lifespan is an exciting reason to want to have a death feigning beetle as a pet. These beetles do have pretty long lifespans for adult beetles. The blue death feigning beetle has been reported to live as long as seventeen years. The author had wild-caught beetles that lived for nine years, so the possibility of a longer maximum lifespan is plausible. Unfortunately, maximum lifespan is not the same as life expectancy or even average lifespan. As a pet owner, we should not go into this thinking we are in for a seventeen-year relationship.

It is more helpful to understand how long a beetle that is wild-caught might be expected to live. In other terms, given a group of beetles, at what time point will half of them still be alive? For different species, the answer differs. In general, it seems like most blue death feigning beetles will still be around for a couple of

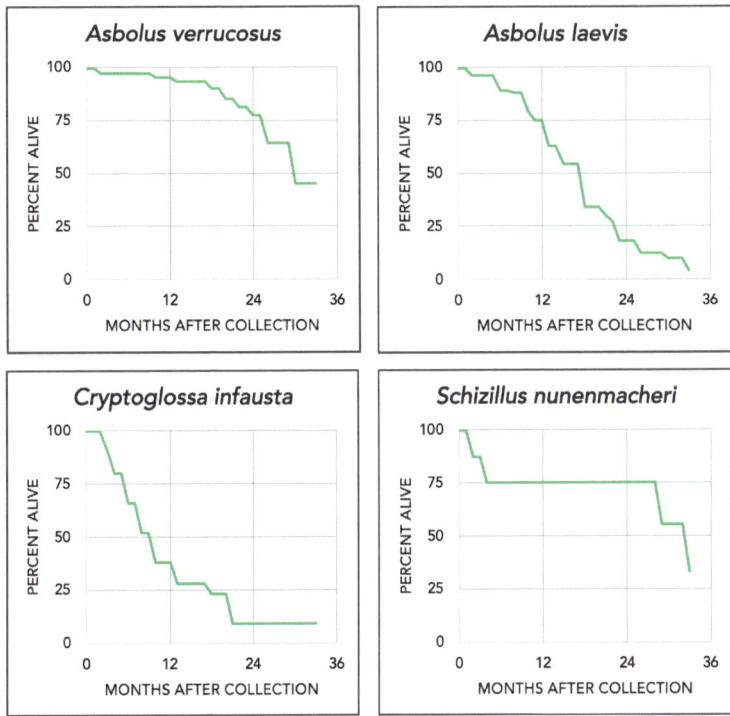

**Figure 5.20**

During their research in the 1980s, the beetle taxonomist Rolf Aalbu created a calendar and noted the months in which wild-caught death feigning beetles died. A portion of that calendar data is uniquely presented here in graphical format to show how long certain beetle species might be expected to live. By following the green line for *Asbolus verrucosus*, you can see that it crosses the 75% alive mark at about 24 months (2 years) after collection and the 50% mark at about 2.5 years. You could expect about half your blue death feigning beetles to be alive after 2.5 years, with some living past that time point. For *Asbolus laevis*, the green line drops much more quickly and the half way mark is at about 18 months (1.5 years). *Cryptoglossa infausta* is a bit less lucky and half of those beetles would be expected to survive less than a year with only about 25% still alive one year after being wild-caught. *Schizillus nunenmacheri* is more like *Asbolus verrucosus* in its longevity (at least within the first three years after collection). There is not enough known to make similar predictions for other species. Maximum lifespans also remain unknown.

years. The "unlucky" death feigning beetle (new common name) might last a little less than a year. There is a need to have more work done monitoring the death times and maximum lifespans of these beetles. People have only studied a few in this manner. In some tenebrionids, males tend to be longer lived than females, but data on death feigning beetles is lacking.

## Parasites and diseases

Because beetles that are for sale as pets are wild-caught, there is the chance that they will have parasites and diseases. This is also true if you collect them for yourself from the wild. The most commonly reported parasites are wasps and flies. Tenebrionids can also suffer from viruses, fungi and bacterial infections. Fortunately, reports on microbial diseases in death feigning beetles are absent or rare. In all cases, there are no methods developed to identify or cure these ailments before it is too late.

Symptoms of a wasp parasite occur shortly before the beetle dies. For braconid wasp parasitism (subfamily Euphorinae), infested beetles will have an uncanny level of activity, running as fast as they can. They will run all around their tank and run into other beetles and objects. It is frenetic. Watch for maggot-like wasp larvae to emerge from the beetle near the tip of the abdomen or the coxae on the legs. If you miss these signs or miss the larvae, they can pupate and become adult wasps. No one has reported on the behavior of beetles parasitized by flies.

A short time before their beetles died, a scientist found fly pupae in the beetle's substrate. These flies were tachinid flies in the genus *Patelloa* (formerly known as *Catagoniopsis*). The only thing you can do against parasites is to stop the next generation. You have to do this by eliminating the parasites that have emerged or by quarantining new pets. The wasp parasites may take longer than a month to emerge from any new arrivals. The fly pupae take about two weeks to develop into flies. There is not enough information at present to really provide guidance on how long to quarantine new arrivals to ensure they are parasite free.

Naturalists have found red mite parasites attached to wild beetles. They are the larvae of either red velvet mites or water mites. They feed on the hemolymph (insect blood) of their hosts. It is unclear if simply removing the mites is sufficient to eliminate them. Any detrimental effects they have on the beetles is unknown.

The following disease symptoms are based on reports in other beetles, not death feigning beetles. The yellow mealworm is a staple tenebrionid in the pet trade. Densovirus infections shut down a commercial operation for many months. The virus-infected larvae showed signs of lethargy. They stopped eating, and displayed odd spinning behavior prior to death. The larvae would generally dehydrate and turn dark.

*Zophobas morio* black wasting virus is a densovirus of superworms. It causes symptoms similar to the densovirus in mealworms. Interestingly, researchers were able to experimentally vaccinate superworms against that disease.

*Beauveria bassiana* is an insecticidal fungus. It kills insects in a matter of days. Symptoms of *Beauveria bassiana* infection are a lack of movement and a white fuzzy surface. *Beauveria bassiana* is somewhat heat sensitive. It does poorly at temperatures above 98°F (37°C).

*Cladosporium* species and *Trichoderma* species are fungi that are being explored as insecticides against tenebrionid beetles too, but their efficacy is low.

Other infections may include bacteria. *Serratia marcescens* may cause immatures to turn pink. Infections with unknown bacteria may cause larvae or pupae to turn black. Sometimes in death feigning beetle cultures, larvae and pupae will die and turn black. It is not clear if a microorganism caused the death. It is possible that the dark color is the result of an opportunistic microorganism that took advantage of the dead corpse.

As previously stated, any ailments that befall a death feigning beetle are likely to be incurable. With a little warning, perhaps you can keep impaired beetles away from the unaffected to prevent further problems.

**Figure 5.21**
Micrograph of an alcohol-preserved parasitic wasp that emerged from a wild-caught death feigning beetle. It is a braconid wasp in the subfamily Euphorinae. These wasps are about 3 millimeters in length.

**Figure 5.22**
This is a tachinid fly in the genus *Patelloa* (*Catagoniopsis*). *Patelloa specularis* was identified as a parasite of *Asbolus verrucosus* and *Asbolus laevis*. Photo by Salvador Vitanza.

**Figure 5.23**
*C. asperata* parasitized by red mites (arrows). Photo by Ana Gatica-Colima. https://www.inaturalist.org/observations/163859048

**Figure 5.24**
Sometimes pupae and larvae die and turn black. It is unclear if the dark melanization is the result of injury or infection.

> <u>Section Summary</u>
> - Death feigning beetles make great pets that are easy to care for
> - You can buy beetles or hunt for them yourself
> - They eat a variety of foods
> - They need moisture
> - They live for a long time
> - You can decorate them with paints and jewels
> - Wild caught specimens may have unknown parasites or diseases

## 6. ADVANCED TECHNIQUES

Are you considering trying to push the existing knowledge base forward, just to see what happens? This is where you'll find experimental methods that may or may not enhance captive breeding. This section is a roadmap, but not a recipe for captive breeding methods. Photographs of some techniques along with explanations of methods are in this section. The text presents the reasoning behind the methods and the modifications that have been proposed. There is also a focus on exposing gaps in knowledge. Experiments that might be worth trying are also discussed. One mealworm company appears to sell captive bred blue death feigning beetles. However, it seems that no one has achieved large scale breeding. Wild-caught specimens are far more abundant and less expensive. So, we still have a strong need for better methods of captive breeding.

A more clear recipe for captive breeding is presented in the next section. I created my original recipe by considering what was already working. I had to ask: "What might make it better?" The experimental process turned to looking at what we knew of the environment in which the insects live. What was missing? Blue death feigning beetles dominate the Mojave Desert. That place is one of the hottest in the world. So, increased temperatures seemed an obvious thing to test. It paid off.

This section is full of mostly anecdotal reports of improvements to the previously existing methods. Some breeders have the good fortune of living where death feigning beetles are abundant. They can make educated guesses on what to do based on what they see in the actual environment. Hobby breeders often have had experiences with many arthropod species. They develop a "gut feeling" for what will make a particular group of organisms thrive. Breeders use this intuition when something fails. Then they make adjustments for their next attempt.

As a breeder, you will have to decide what success means to you. In an ideal world, you would make side-by-side comparisons of different conditions. You have to do this to demonstrate their effectiveness. You won't be certain that your new methods are actually making an impact unless others can repeat them. This means describing them in enough detail that others can replicate them.

## Sex Determination

If you want to successfully breed death feigning beetles, you need to have adult males and females. The primary characteristic in *Asbolus* males is hairy antennae. Females have less hairy antennae. No, the ladies don't shave their antennae! For *Cryptoglossa*, the males possess tubercles on the mesofemurs. These are absent in females. Three exceptions are *C. bicostata*, *C. infausta* and *C. seriata*. Males of those three species lack the tubercles. Interestingly, those three species share more characteristics with *Asbolus* and *Schizillus* than the other six *Cryptoglossa* species. In fact, *C. infausta* was almost assigned to the genus *Asbolus* when it was first discovered.

Among *C. infausta* specimens, there are clearly individuals with hairy antennae and individuals without. Pairing beetles together showed that the beetle with hairy antenna was mounting the one with less hairy antennae. This indicates that they are like *Asbolus* when it comes to sexual dimorphism. The couple produced offspring. You can use the antennae for sex determination in *C. infausta*.

People have posted photos of *Schizillus* species online that show individuals with both hairy and non-hairy antennae. This suggests sex differences within *Schizillus* also might be the same as in *Asbolus*.

There are death feigning beetles that are difficult to sex. You can watch for mounting behavior as a reasonable way to tell if you have males in your population. It does not guarantee that the recipient of the male's attention is a female or of the same species! Many male death-feigning beetles do not seem to be too fussy. Egg laying certainly would identify females.

**Figure 6.1**
Sex determination using antennae in *Asbolus*. Examples of female (top) and male (bottom) antennae for *Asbolus verrucosus*.

**Figure 6.2**
Examples of female (top) and male (bottom) antennae for *Asbolus laevis*.

**Figure 6.3**
Sex determination in the genus *Cryptoglossa*. Female mesofemur (top) and male mesofemur (bottom) for *C. variolosa*. The male femur possesses a tubercle on the lower side near the base.

**Figure 6.4**
Sex determination in the genus *Cryptoglossa*. Female mesofemur (top) and male mesofemur (bottom) for *C. variolosa*. The tubercle is a bit less obvious in this specimen.

**Figure 6.5**
Sex determination in the genus *Cryptoglossa*. Female mesofemur (top) and male mesofemur (bottom) for *C. variolosa*. Another specimen where the tubercle is less prominent but visible as a dark region.

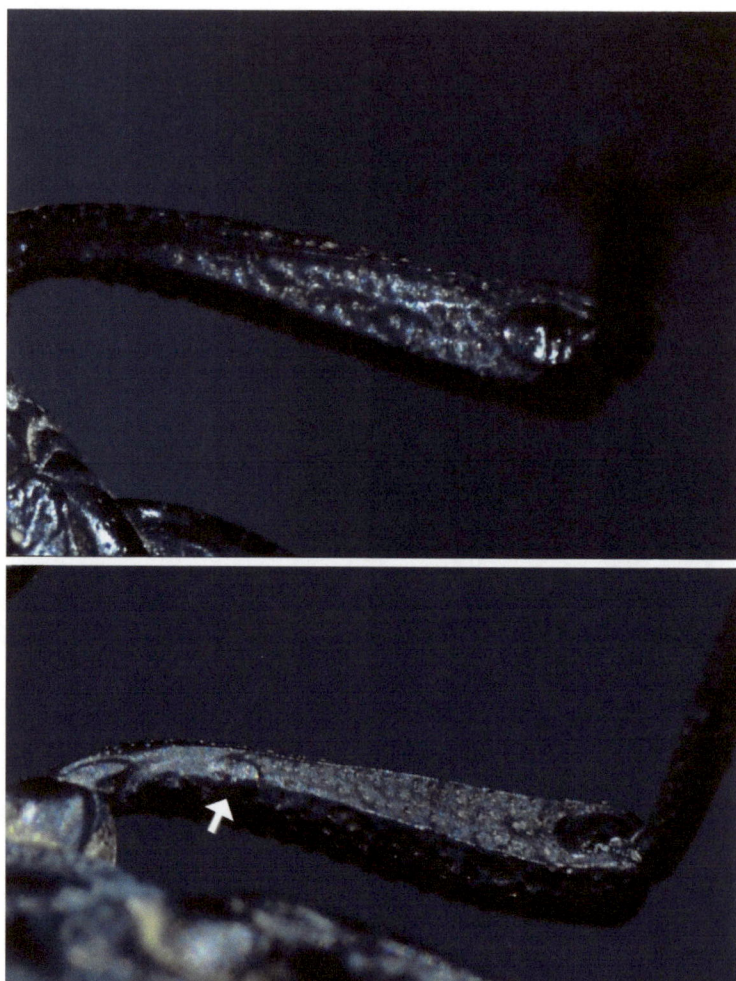

**Figure 6.6**
Sex determination in the genus *Cryptoglossa*. Female mesofemur (top) and male mesofemur (bottom) for *C. muricata*. The male femur possesses a tubercle on the lower side near the base.

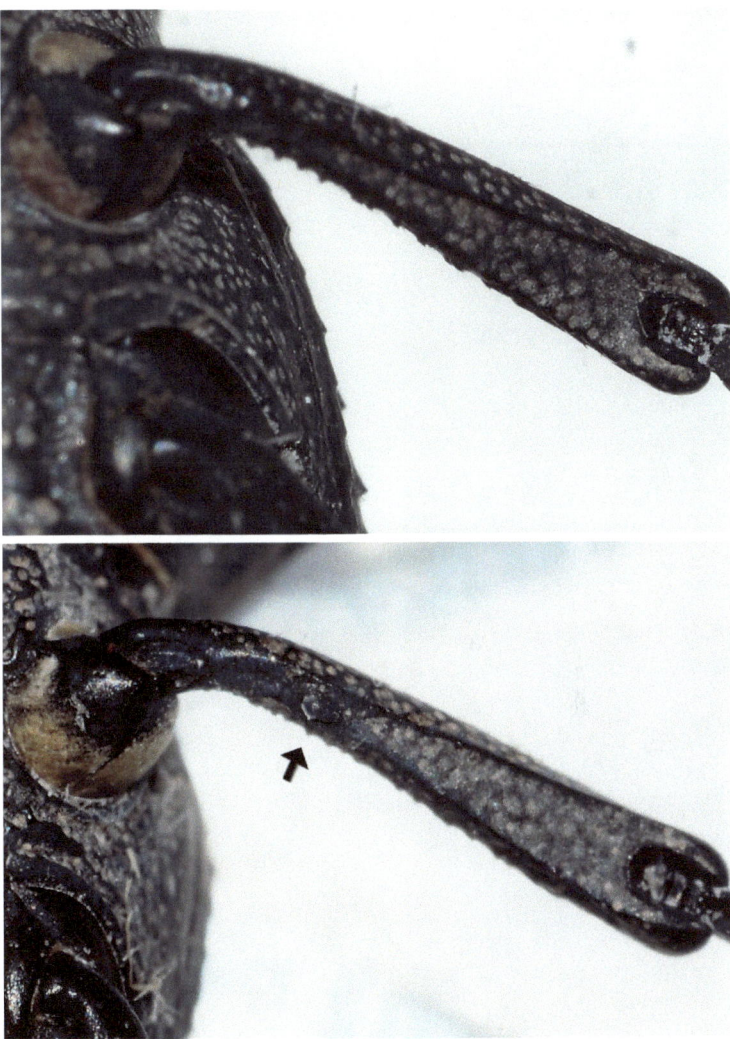

**Figure 6.7**
Sex determination in the genus *Cryptoglossa*. Female mesofemur (top) and male mesofemur (bottom) for *C. muricata*. The male femur possesses a tubercle on the lower side near the base.

**Figure 6.8**
Examples of presumed female (top) and male (bottom) antennae for *Cryptoglossa infausta*. The pair shown here produced larvae a few months after their photos were taken. They were housed in a setup like those shown in figure 5.5.

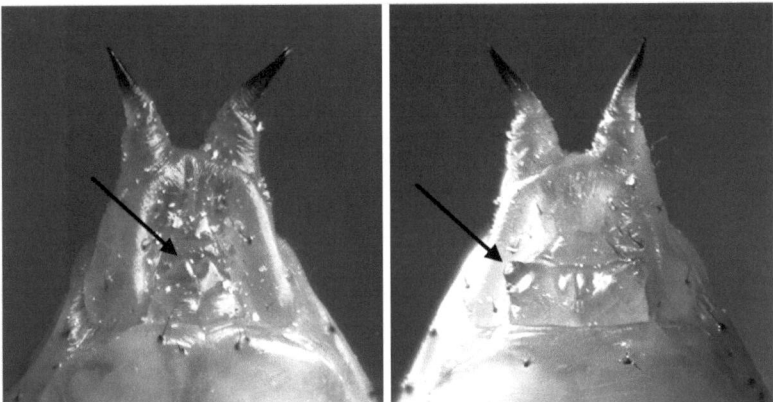

**Figure 6.9**
Sex determination in tenebrionid pupae. Here, *Tenebrio molitor* is being used as an example. This is the yellow mealworm. The male is on the left and the female is on the right. The male structure has two small bumps (arrow). The female structure is similar but also has horn-like structures (arrow). Death feigning beetles are similar in appearance except that female horn-like structures are longer.

This section presents examples of sex differences for *Asbolus* and *Cryptoglossa*. It includes multiple examples to show different angles and variation. You probably need some type of magnification (microscope) to identify male *Cryptoglossa* by their tubercles. This is not necessary for those species whose antennae are diagnostic. Simply holding the insects between yourself and a distant light source will reveal the fringe on the back-lit antennae. It helps to close one eye. With practice, this becomes easier.

In pupae, sex is easy to determine by the structures after the seventh sternite. Like other tenebrionids, females possess what looks like the rock and roll/horned hand gesture. The structure in males is a small, hornless (2 knuckle) version. Of course, you need pupae to examine. If you get that far, you are already a rock star!

## Containers

If you plan to house larvae individually, you will probably need a lot of containers. Some breeders use soufflé cups. Mature larvae will pupate on the surface or in shallow containers if they must.

**Figure 6.10**
To save space, soufflé cups can be used to house individual larvae as they grow. Ventilation is made by piercing the sides of the cup multiple times around the perimeter with an insect pin using the same technique used for watering straws. In this example a single larvula was placed into a cup with a highly organic sand mix and a piece of kibble. A lid was then placed onto the container after the photo was taken.

Most prefer to go as deep into substrate as they can before creating a pupal cell. Soufflé cups are relatively inexpensive. Restaurant supply vendors often offer the lowest prices. These tiny cups with lids are not suitable for immediate use. You have to make holes in them with a pin to allow ventilation. A single soufflé cup might need thirty tiny holes placed around the perimeter to allow for ventilation of tenebrionid larvae. It might help to perforate the lid too. The soufflé cups take up much less space than other containers. However, you have to monitor for moldy food or drying substrate more often with these small cups. If you have a small incubator, you can try to pupate a few larvae at a time. While those larvae are being induced to pupate in larger containers, you can continue to use these small cups to keep your other larvae. You can do this for quite a while, as long as you maintain ventilation and a clean environment for the larvae. Experiments have shown that mature blue death feigning beetle larvae kept up to 3 months after maturation are still able to be induced to pupate. Therefore, you can induce pupation in small batches of larvae. You can repeat the process for all your larvae over a longer period of time.

Taller containers that allow for larval development and pupation can range in price considerably, depending on your preferences. On the lowest end, free is possible. Ask people in your network to save their water bottles. Ask them to give the bottles to you instead of recycling them or throwing them in the trash. Small 16 oz (473 ml) water bottles work well. Use scissors to cut off the tops. On the opposite end of the cost spectrum are acrylic boxes. These may be a couple of dollars each, depending on the source. They are very nice if you want to see clearly when a pupal cell has been made. They are also good if you want to monitor the progress of the larva-to-adult transition. Plastic bottles made of polypropylene are mid-range in price. The most important property is that the container accommodates the substrate and the insects. If you use shallow cups like deli cups, make sure they have lids that allow for ventilation but do not allow insects to escape. Taller containers with 2-3 inches (4-6 cm) of smooth wall above the substrate will prevent escapes without the need for lids.

For group housing, containers that offer more area, rather than depth are beneficial. These can range from used take out containers to baseball card boxes, critter cages, plastic shoe boxes and aquariums. It does not require a huge commitment of space to get eggs. A 2.5 gallon tank or shoe box has enough surface area for egg laying. In short, you need a variety of containers for different reasons.

## Sand and coconuts

Sand is the basis for all the substrates used here and in the standard recipe. Play sand from any of the home improvement stores should work. It is usually available in 50 pound (22.6 kg) bags for a few dollars. My early tests used pure sand. Coir was added to make the moisture last longer. Coir is also known as coco coir. It is a substrate made from the pith and fibers of coconut husks. It is available in many pet stores and comes as a solid brown block that you have to soak in water to expand. Once it is expanded, you can let it dry out again and remove any large pieces or long fibers before mixing it with sand. Coir is also available as loose material in bags. I normally use a 1:1 sand to coir mix (by volume). That basically means one scoop of sand and one scoop of coir. The 1:1 sand to coir mix is referred to as "standard substrate".

## Half in

Pet beetle owners may desire to have a nice display tank and simultaneously have the possibility of breeding beetles in captivity. This kind of "half in" approach leads many toward a multipart substrate setup. You can use multipart substrates as a way of meeting your aesthetic desires while meeting the needs of different life stages. You also can do this if you want to avoid monitoring egg hatching or separating the larvae from the adults.

There are two methods that people commonly employ. The first method involves setting up an aquarium with sandy soil. Carve out a corner and place a more organic soil in that location. Then regularly water that corner. Organic in this context means it contains biological material that is potentially of nutritional value - like leaves and rotting wood or bark and compost. The idea behind this method is that the adults will lay eggs in the sandy area. Then the larvae will find their way to the corner with better soil and moisture where they will continue their development. The benefit of such an arrangement is your ability to dig around in the substrate of the corner region to search for mature larvae and

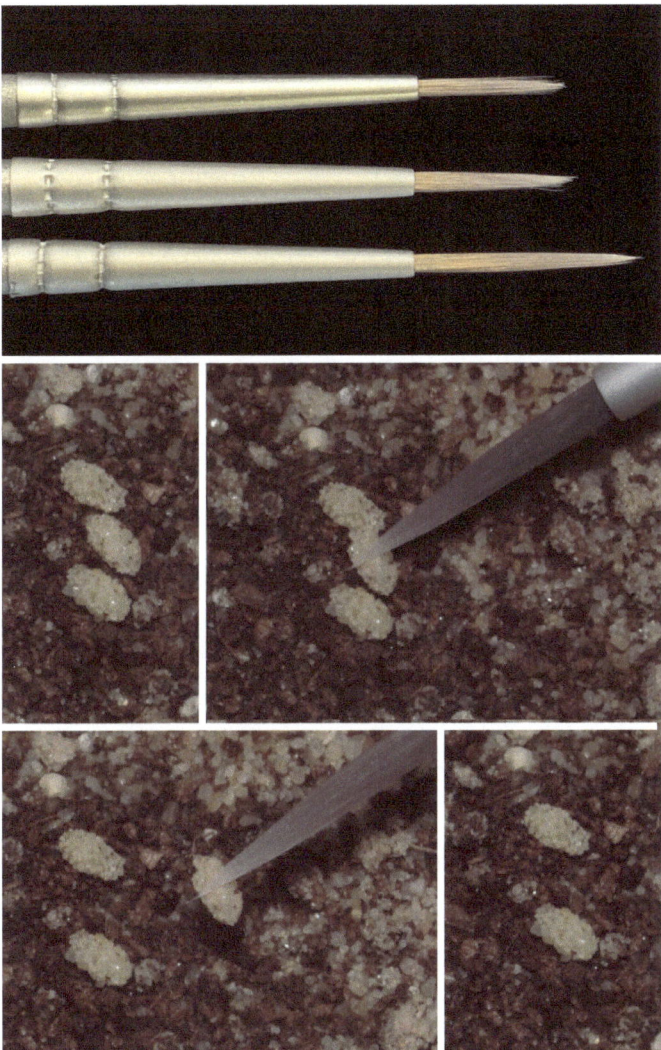

**Figure 6.11**
Paintbrushes (top row) include a 0 round, 1 round and a 1 liner (from top to bottom). Eggs floating with coir on top of sand (middle row - left) before an egg was selected by touching it with a moist round size 1 brush (middle row - right). The egg has been lifted (bottom left) and moved to elsewhere (missing egg - bottom right).

**Figure 6.12**
Benefits of staging larvae. Larvae at similar ages can be grouped and their growth monitored over time. Similarly sized larvae may survive better when housed in a group than mixed sized larvae would.

**Figure 6.13**
Captive bred blue death feigning beetles.

move them to another location for further development (to induce pupation).

An alternative approach is to use a multi-layered substrate. You prepare a lower layer made with more organic materials and an upper layer made with sand. Combined with improved methods of delivering water to the lower layer, the second approach has an advantage. Hatched larvae will follow their natural instinct to dig downward, and they do not have to go very far to find organic material. A disadvantage to this approach is that to maintain the aesthetic and still collect larvae, you must remove the upper layer and put it back later.

Because both systems usually have sand arenas for egg laying, you can still sift the sand. You can collect eggs and larvae from those areas. At least one tenebrionid breeder has suggested that the presence of larvae stimulates beetles to lay eggs. By placing larvae in a tank of beetles that are otherwise not reproducing, you may get them to start. Using yellow mealworms can help, but it has been suggested that more closely related species are more effective. This is an interesting concept. It lends itself to housing multiple species together, especially if one is easy to breed and another is more difficult.

## Stratifying immatures

This section is going to cover some techniques for collecting eggs and small larvae. It will cover how to move them from one container to another. The purpose of collecting eggs and stratifying larvae is to prevent cannibalism. There is limited evidence that this is absolutely required. At least when you keep individual larvae in separate containers, it guarantees that another larva cannot injure or eat them. Stratifying larvae into similarly aged groups or instars during group housing ensures that larvae are more able to defend themselves from cannibalism. Imagine if a hungry older larva stops by and finds a freshly molted first instar larva that fits easily into its mandibles. Who would win that fight?

Females prefer sandy substrates for egg laying. Sifting sand or standard substrate is the easiest way to collect the eggs. You want the sand or substrate mix to be able to pass through the sifter and leave behind only eggs. This is why the standard breeding protocol in the next chapter mentions sifting the substrate before sterilizing the substrate and using it. You will have already tossed out the bigger particles so they do not interfere with egg collection.

When sifting sand for eggs and larvae, it is important to only collect the dry sand from the upper surface because the moist or wet sand will clog the screen of the sieve. For species that are ok with laying eggs in fine dry sand like *A. verrucosus* and *A. laevis*, you can house adults in a tank or tub that has only dry sand as a substrate. This provides benefits for egg collection but also requires you to collect eggs and larvae and move them to more suitable habitats for growth.

Sifters or sieves come in standard sizes. These standard "mesh sizes" exist so everybody can repeat what other people are doing when it comes to particle size selection. The size that works very well for eggs is ASTM standard mesh No. 16 (1.18 millimeters). The No. 20 (0.841 millimeters) also works well. The mesh size is referring to the space between the wires. The company that makes the sieve is not that important because this mesh spacing is an agreed upon standard. It is also not that important if you choose stainless steel versus brass. You can get sifters in different diameters and heights. A convenient size is 8 inches in diameter (203 millimeters) with 2-5/8 inch depth (66 millimeters; also known as full height). This allows you to sift 2-3 cups (0.4-0.7 liter) of sand at a time. The ring that holds the mesh is part of a complete setup. There is an option to also buy a bottom pan for collecting the substrate material that falls through. You don't need a bottom pan, but it is convenient to have if you have no place to collect your substrate. You can find these items online from a variety of companies. Look at vendors catering to soil analysis. The prices vary widely and if this is something that seems to be too expensive, there are ways to collect eggs without using a screen.

A non-sifting method involves collecting a small amount of dry substrate that may contain eggs or larvae. Place it into a large pan or on a paper plate. Then shake the pan or plate from side to

# DEATH FEIGNING BEETLES | 113

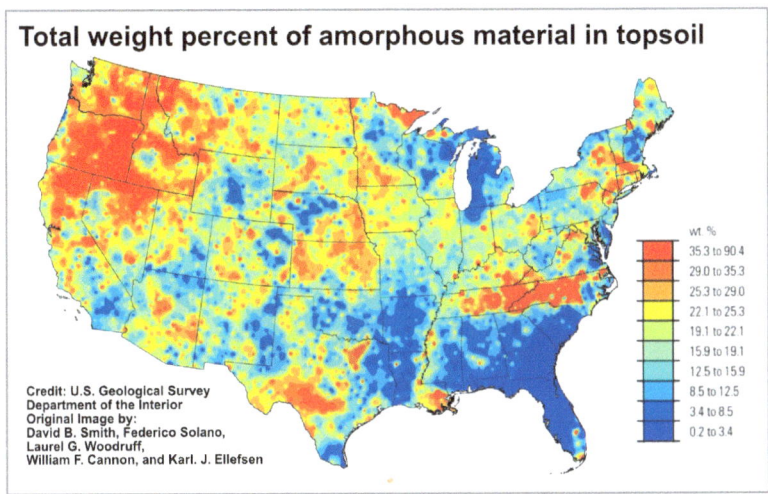

**Figure 6.14**
Intensity map depicting the total weight percent of amorphous material in topsoil in the United States. Amorphous material is anything that was not identified as a mineral and can be considered as an approximation of the organic material present. In the regions where sand dunes are present (like the southeastern tip of California), there is very little amorphous material. This is blue. In western Texas, it can exceed 25%. This is orange. Thus, one might expect dune-loving species to prefer less organic material while others may require more.

side (not up and down) to spread the substrate out into a thin layer (like panning for gold). The thinness of the substrate layer will help eggs stand out because they will be taller than the particles of sand. They are also less dense than the sand and will "float" on top even if you cannot get the layer spread out very thin. Other low-density particles will also be present, like coir and food particles (e.g. seeds and cricket bits). So, you will be in a position where you can see the eggs, but now you have to be able to pick them up and move them without crushing them. Sometimes this same problem occurs with sifted eggs, especially if your substrate has a lot of debris from food scattered about in the tank.

The method for picking up eggs and small larvae without crushing them uses a paintbrush moistened with water. This technique works very well. It is not uncommon for entomologists

### Figure 6.15

Organic material being tested. A commercially available Asbolus Substrate (top) contains a variety of organic materials. After sifting, larger materials appeared to include leaf litter (possibly live oak leaves; middle row - left), shredded bark (middle row - center), and gravel (middle row - right). These items were not removed during the test. After months in group culture, many of the larvae remained alive (bottom) and were transferred to individual housing for pupation.

to use this technique to collect specimens in the field. In the absence of a source of water, many are compelled to lick the hairs on the brush to moisten them. A safer method is to use a water-filled cap from a water bottle and just dip the brush in the water whenever needed.

With the moistened bristles, lightly touch the center of the egg. It should immediately stick to the brush through capillary action, and you can lift the egg to a new container. Frequently, you will pick up small debris in the vicinity of the egg. This is acceptable. Trying to release the egg by brushing it into the new substrate can be frustrating. Sometimes you can crush an egg trying to get it to release. The easiest way to release the egg from the brush is to tap the brush handle against the edge of the new container while suspending the bristles over the new substrate. The inertia of the egg will fling it off of the bristles and into the new container. The same method works for small larvae.

The size and type of brush is important. A "camel-hair brush" is usually suggested, but in reality, no one makes them from camel's hair. Supposedly they are squirrel hair and one premium brush style uses Siberian Kolinsky sable hair. There are other types that will work. It can be synthetic or natural hair. What you want to find and use in this situation is what they call either a round type or a liner type of paintbrush. The size for round can be from 5/0, to a 0 or 1. Size 2 is getting towards oversized. Liners are like rounds with longer bristles. A size 0 or 1 for a liner is probably a good choice. Artists use these brushes with watercolor and acrylic paints. If the hairs become bent or frayed, the brush is pretty useless. Some vendors package the brushes with a protective cap. These are sometimes difficult to place on the brush without damaging the bristles. To prevent damage, store the brush in a protected place laying on its side, or in a cup with the bristle end upwards.

## Organic substrates

The standard substrate was designed to mimic the methods of other successful breeders. They did the bulk of their research in the early 1980s. Their main focus was research on larval forms of the beetles. Their substrate was pure sand. Sand is still the preferred substrate for egg laying. The reason behind the addition of coir to the mix for blue death feigning beetles was two-fold. I believed that it would help maintain moisture and thought that if larvae were desperate, they might find coir to be edible.

Coir is promoted for its ability to increase moisture in sandy soils. The time it takes for the substrate to dry out is longer with coir present. However, the sand and coir in the mixes both dry out together. The coir does not seem to retain its moisture when surrounded by dry sand. The relative pith to fiber content of the coir also influences the moisture retaining ability of the material. More fiber is less capable of water retention. Unfortunately, coir seems to have little nutritive value. Coir and sand, at least, did not rot or decay. Substrates still needed improvement.

There are some tenebrionid aficionados who swear by using soil and wood-based substrates with leaf litter for all tenebrionids. This is probably not the best approach for desert beetles. Pure sand may not be the best approach either. Successful breeders of death feigning beetles indicated that the desert floor comprises more than sand. Because of this, they incorporate a good portion of other materials into their substrate mixes. If you look back at the soil samples from chapter 3, you can see a few bits of grass and other plants in those samples.

It is true that most desert soils are a mixture of sand and other materials. The mixture contains organic materials. It also has minerals that are coarser (gravel) and minerals that are more fine (clay). Desert soils are most often described as sandy loam or loamy sand. Unsurprisingly, the amount of organic material in the deserts of North America is concentrated near plants and is less concentrated as you move further away from plants. Multiple breeders have been implementing sand that they mix with organic materials, especially materials that might serve as a food source. A setup for breeding beetles can sometimes veer away from what one might consider aesthetically pleasing. What looks good in a display tank may not be compatible with what's best for breeding.

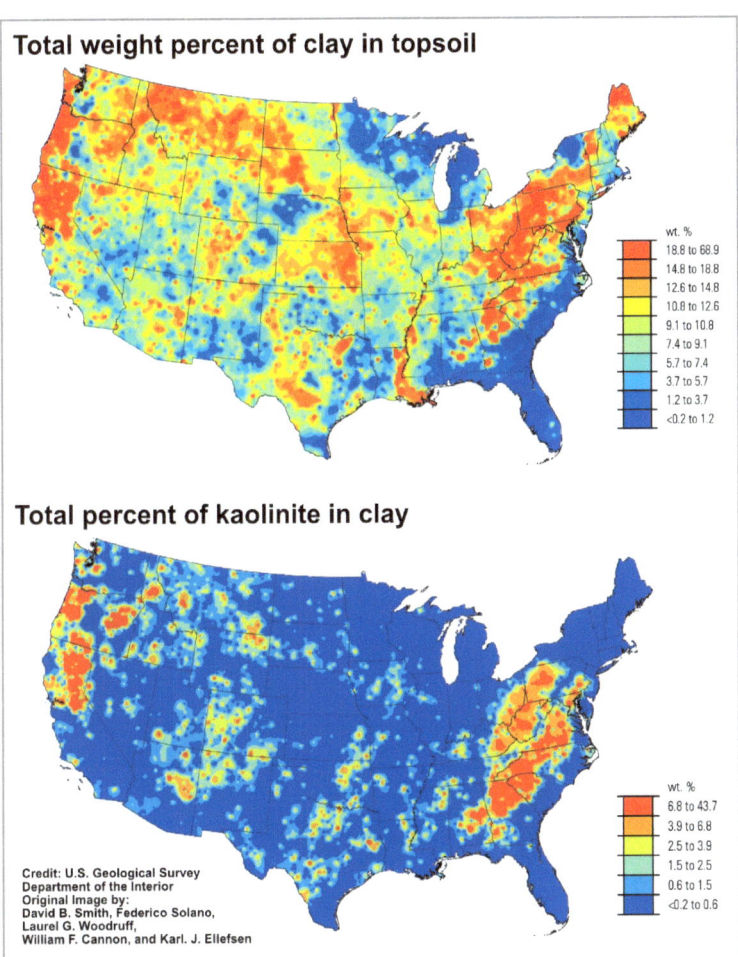

**Figure 6.16**

Intensity maps depicting the total weight percent of clay in topsoil in the United States (top) and the weight percent of kaolinite in clay (bottom). In the regions where death feigning beetles live, clay percentages are normally below 12% (blue to light orange on the top map) with less than 0.6% kaolinite (blue in the bottom map). This indicates they are bentonite-like clays.

The types and amounts of organic materials can vary. A fermented wood mixture called flake soil serves as the base for many invertebrate soil recipes. In particular, millipede mixes, pill bug mixes, and beetle mixes. These mixes often contain potting soil, peat moss, sphagnum moss, and crushed leaves as well as many other trace ingredients. The main goal in adding these to substrate mixes is to provide some form of decaying plant matter for larvae. Unless you are keen on developing your own organic mixes, it is probably faster and less expensive to purchase small amounts of different organic substrates from reputable suppliers. It is relatively easy to purchase one of these and mix it with sand.

The optimal ratio of organic material to sand is not clear as no one has reported side-by-side testing of different mixes. However, such "dirt-sand" mixes can be reasonably high on the "dirt" side and still seem to work well. Additionally, no magic bullet for the best type of organic mix has been reported. There are reports that spent roach substrates and spent millipede substrates can stimulate egg laying in species that were reluctant to breed.

A two-part commercial product called "Asbolus Substrate" recently became available for hobbyists. One part is sand. It comes in a separate bag. The other part is a proprietary organic mix. The organic mix appears to be composed of potting soil, leaf litter, and shredded bark. The author tested the organic part of Asbolus Substrate by combining it with the standard substrate. One fourth was composed of organic Asbolus Substrate and three fourths was the original recipe standard substrate (by dry volume). Larvae of blue death feigning beetles reared in this environment performed well. They matured in a group setting, suggesting that cannibalism gets reduced when there is suitable organic material in the substrate. Mushroom mix compost gave similar results. This line of testing needs more work.

## Clay

Clay has been proposed as a substrate amendment during pupal cell formation for certain species of death feigning beetle. The main problem was that pupal cells constructed in sand may

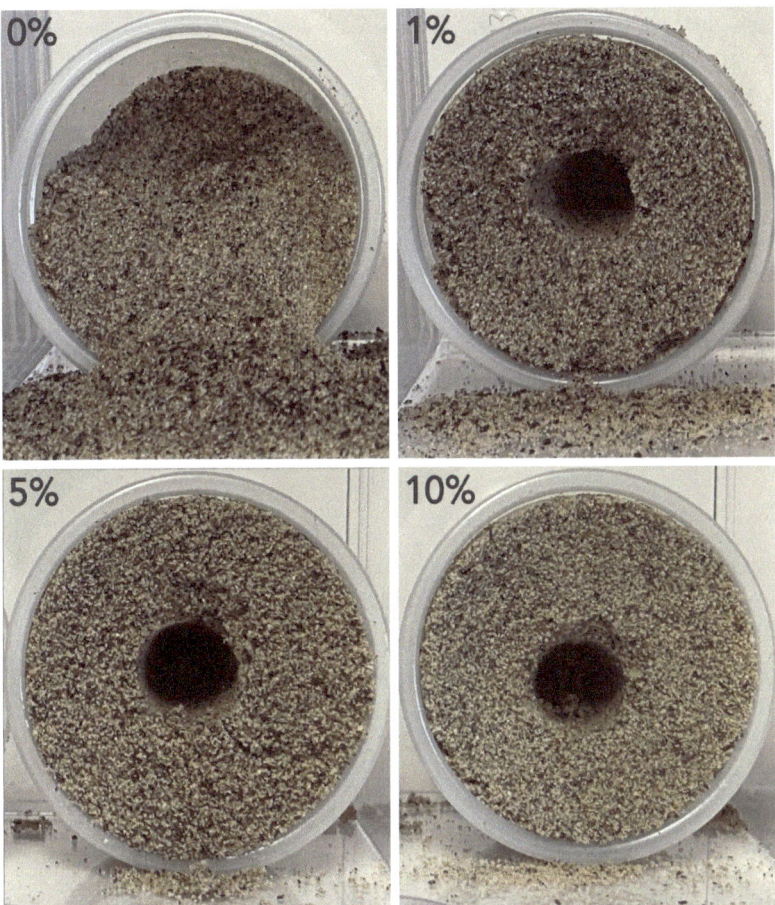

**Figure 6.17**
Artificial pupal cells made in sand with increasing amounts of clay from 0%, 1%, 5% and 10% are shown after air drying for 36 hours. Note that the sample without clay (0%) has collapsed and the amount of debris that has fallen gets lower with increasing clay content. The 5% and 10% samples retained their shape when fully dried.

dry out and the dry sand then collapses. You can prevent this by keeping up with the bottom watering. This is a time-consuming step if you have hundreds of individual containers. Additionally, *Asbolus mexicanus mexicanus* performs poorly when kept in high humidity. To overcome this, amending the soil with small amounts of clay can be beneficial. Clay increases the cohesiveness of soil. Thus, the addition of clay to a sandy substrate would be consistent with maintaining the shape of the pupal cell. Clay will keep shape even if the cell dries out slightly between watering events. There are different clay types. There are what are known as 1:1 clays (kaolinite and halloysite) and 2:1 clays (illite and montmorillonite). They impart different levels of strength to sandy soils. While clay sometimes exceeds 10 percent (by weight) of the topsoil in the desert, less than 0.6 percent (by weight) is the kaolinite type of clay. This means desert clays are mostly bentonite-like (montmorillonite) clay.

With a bit of knowledge about the natural environment of the beetles, and realizing there is a need to test the use of clay, I did an experiment with clay. Clay was added to the standard substrate. This was done to see how much clay improved the stability of the substrate when it dries. Small batches of standard substrate (50 grams) were amended with bentonite clay from the Mojave Desert. This was done in amounts of 0%, 1%, 5%, and 10% (by dry weight). A small amount of water (2 milliliters; 0.067 oz) was added and the sample was thoroughly mixed to form a near homogenous substrate that was capable of forming clumps.

Rather than waiting to test the mix on beetle larvae, pupal cells were simulated. To simulate a pupal cell, each mix was packed into a small deli cup (3/4 oz; 22 ml). An impression was made in the center of the substrate using the end of a permanent marking pen. The simulated pupal cells were then turned sideways and allowed to air dry. As expected, the standard substrate collapsed upon drying. All three clay mixtures held shape better. The 10% clay mix retained its shape the best.

In terms of mixing by volume instead of weight, this 10% mix was about 4 parts standard substrate and 1 part clay. Interestingly, this same volumetric ratio is used by some beetle breeders to create a substrate for pupation of goliath beetle grubs.

From the data on soil composition in the desert, and experiments with synthetic pupal cells, it is clear that when clay is present in amounts observed in nature, it promotes structural

**Figure 6.18**
Marbles (top left), a 1.5 inch PVC pipe cut to the depth of the substrate and a koi pond filter that is cut to fit the bottom of the tank (top right) represent the system. The assembled system (bottom) is shown at a point when the substrate has been partially filled in.

**Figure 6.19**
Breaking wide-bore straws free from the plaster casting.

stability. Outside of the work reported for *A. mexicanus*, it remains to be determined how much clay (if any) is optimal for other death feigning beetles. It may be worthwhile to experiment with different amounts of bentonite or montmorillonite (desert types) of clay amendments. It would be good to optimize the results for different species of death feigning beetles when they form their pupal cells.

More work needs to be done to improve substrates and optimize them for the different life stages of the various species. However, it is not clear what the best measurement of success should be. One breeder may choose to separate larvae at a young age, one may separate mature larvae for pupation, and another may just wait to see if they get any beetles from a mixed population. The breeders that separate larvae early seem to be able to produce adults.

If this were an ecology class, whatever produced the most reproductive females in the shortest amount of time would be the winning combination. However, we also like larger and longer lived beetles. To move the captive breeding of death feigning beetles forward, we need several things. Being able to mass rear larvae in the same container by finding ways of preventing cannibalism would vastly reduce the cost and the labor involved. Reductions in both are likely needed to make captive breeding a competitive option for the pet trade. If larvae can be induced to pupate without the need for separate housing, this would also be an amazing advancement.

## Water

Despite being desert beetles capable of surviving for relatively long periods without water, water is a critical aspect of raising death feigning beetles in captivity. Adults and immatures need water. They can often get it from food. It helps to supplement food with water access. To make a drinking waterer for adult beetles, fill a pill bottle or similar tube-like container with water and plug it with two cotton balls. Fifty milliliter (1.7 ounce) conical bottom test tubes also work well for this purpose. The plugged

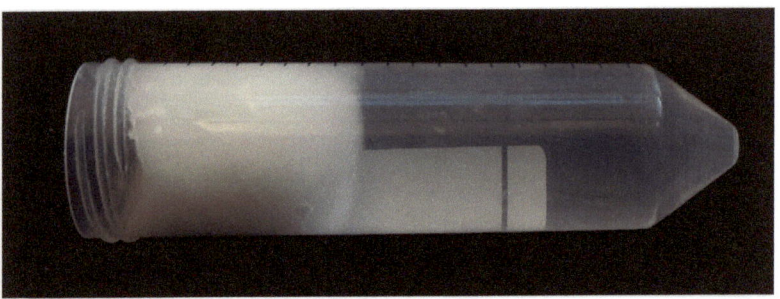

**Figure 6.20**
A test tube waterer.

tube, when laid on its side, allows beetles access to water to drink without the risk of drowning. Different species are also sometimes found hiding in these tubes, perhaps to stay in a slightly more humid environment.

A sandy substrate with a moisture gradient can stimulate egg laying in some species. It seems unnecessary for inducing egg laying in others. Habitats set up for egg laying or larval development can benefit from having a moisture gradient. This works well where the lower substrate has greater levels of moisture.

Researchers originally generated a moisture gradient for larvae using a plaster lower layer. They housed individual larvae in 8-ounce cups (237 milliliters) where plaster was cast in the bottom. They stuck an upright straw in the plaster and put a layer of sand over the plaster. The straw allowed them to add water to the plaster below the sand. This created a moisture gradient in the sand. Larger versions were made with plastic shoe boxes and were used for egg-laying adults. However, this was a relatively expensive setup for individual larvae and the absorption of water into plaster was unbearably slow. To overcome these limitations, a great deal of experimentation was done.

It was far faster to skip embedding straws into plaster for delivering water to the lower substrate. Larvae would frequently enter the bottom of the straw and become trapped. Sometimes they would make their way up the straw and out of their enclosure. Straws are also inadequate for large enclosures. Aquarium-sized

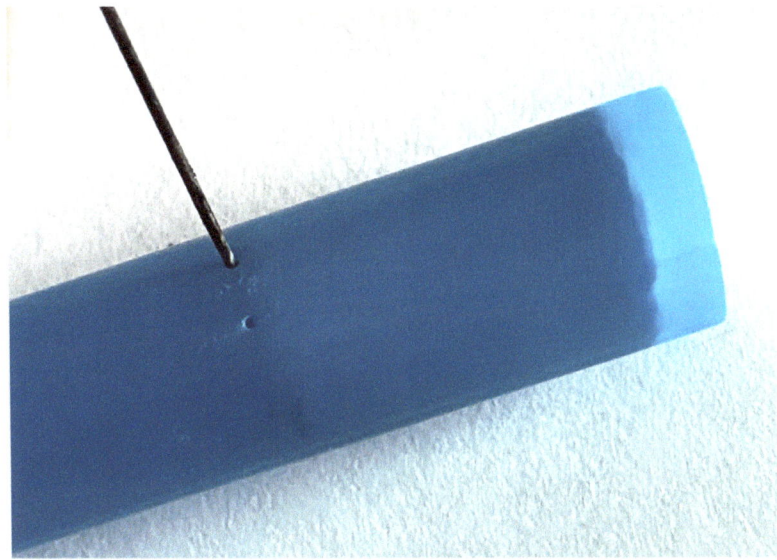

**Figure 6.21**
Demonstration of the use of an insect pin to poke holes in the wide-bore straw just above the plaster plug. The same method is used to create ventilation in 2 oz deli cups.

habitats used underground drip hoses. Again, the delivery of water to the lower substrate was still relatively slow. The following text provides methods that offer lower costs, rapid delivery of water to the lower substrate, and they protect from the perils of open-ended tubes.

To make an aquarium-sized bottom waterer, the materials required include a koi pond fiber filter, a piece of pipe and marbles. The filter pad is about ½ inch or 12 mm thick. Cut it to fit the bottom of the aquarium. The filter becomes the lowest portion of the setup and functions in the same manner as the plaster used in older setups. It is not a rubber-type material and should not have open spaces big enough for sand to fall through or into the filter pad. However, being highly porous, the filter allows water to spread out across the bottom of the tank very rapidly. Instead of a straw, use 1.5 inch (38.1 millimeter) PVC pipe. Cut the pipe to a length equal to the planned depth of

**Figure 6.22**
Assembling individual containers to house single larvae, pupae and teneral adults. Containers are presented that have lower (left), intermediate (middle) and higher (right) costs (top left image). The wide-bore watering straw is placed inside the container with the plugged end downward (top right image) before substrate is added. The completed housing is presented at the bottom.

substrate. This pipe will allow you to pour a large volume of water into the system filter in a short period of time. While it is more expensive than cutting pipe to length, a 1.5 inch (38.1 millimeter) PVC coupling can be used. They are a standard size that is just about right for substrate depth and they have clean, parallel edges. The marbles are used to fill the pipe. These prevent beetles from

**Figure 6.23**
The wide-bore straws help make delivering water more rapid when using a pump bottle that has a hose attached. The upper substrate is lighter and drier than the lower substrate.

falling into the watering hole. You can use similarly-sized rocks to fill the PVC pipe. There still needs to be a large volume of airspace between the rocks to allow water to flow rapidly. Avoid using small rocks or sand to fill this space. Once substrate is added to the system, you can bottom water.

To overcome the negatives of plaster, but maintain the positives for individual housing, plaster plugged wide-bore straws (milk shake straws) are now used. To generate plaster plugs, first mix up an amount of plaster sufficient to cover the bottom of a relatively deep container with about a centimeter (½ inch or 10 mm) of plaster. In the example presented here, I used a critter cage. A pie pan or similar container could also be used. Before the plaster hardens, embed the ends of straws into the plaster. When the plaster has hardened, break the straws free from the casting. Each wide-bore straw will have its own plaster plug. The plug's purpose is to prevent larvae from getting into the straw. To facilitate rapid release of water into the bottom of the substrate, make small holes in the straw just above the plaster plug. Four holes at roughly 90 degrees apart works well but more can be included. The straws can be cut to the height of the rearing containers. You can make housing for individuals that has bottom watering. Place one of the straws in the container with the plaster end down and fill the container with substrate. Avoid filling the straw with substrate. Bottom watering is easily and rapidly achieved using a pump bottle with a small hose attached.

## Food

Food was covered briefly in the Bestest Pets section. One thing that has not really been addressed is why certain choices are made and what future directions might be interesting to pursue.

The food used in the standard protocol in the next chapter is based on research papers that described the gut contents of death feigning beetles. Researchers dissected wild-caught beetles. They quantified the identities of the items inside. Insects comprised about 60% of the gut contents. Blue death feigning beetles readily consumed dead insects that they received as food. This solidified the use of dead, dried crickets as a food source. Carrots served as a source of moisture and were really a carry over from using carrots for rearing mealworms. By keeping this diet as simple as possible, it created opportunities for later improvement. Before this, other studies used grains and seeds for breeding death feigning beetles. One study used cabbage as the sole food source. Other contemporary beetle enthusiasts use dog chow almost exclusively for tenebrionid beetles. There is no legitimate reason to restrict the diet to crickets and carrots. You can save quite a bit

**Figure 6.24**
Food sources can vary considerably. The original protocol for blue death feigning beetles used crickets and carrots (top row) as standard food items, while previous researchers used seeds and grains (middle row - left). Seed/grain mixes (wild bird seed) can be ground in a coffee grinder (middle right) to make smaller particles that are easier for the insects to use. Many beetle enthusiasts use kibble for cats and dogs (bottom right) as a staple food source. The last sample is creosote bush leaves, which contain a life-extending chemical abbreviated as NDGA.

on food costs by using kibble. Despite the members of the genus *Asbolus* preferring dead dried insects, these beetles will consume a wide variety of foods. There are currently no food types that are known to cause harm to death feigning beetles. However, many

**Figure 6.25**
A creosote bush - *Larrea tridentata*, also known as chaparral.

people try to avoid potential pesticides by choosing organic vegetables. One bit of caution is that there are organic pesticides. Garlic, Bt, and pyrethrum are examples. So, organic does not mean pesticide free. There is no specific beetle food that is known to enhance captive breeding or to produce larger or longer-lived beetles. That does not mean we cannot try to find some... like broccoli.

Yep, that green vegetable called broccoli. In the red flour beetle (another tenebrionid beetle), adding broccoli into the diet resulted in a 30% increase in average lifespan. Broccoli contains an antioxidant called sulforaphane. Sulforaphane is believed to be the compound responsible for life extension. So, formulating a diet for beetles that included broccoli powder might prove to be fruitful for extending lifespan, especially for captive bred beetles. There are commercially available pet foods made with poultry and a small amount of broccoli. Unfortunately at least one of those products does contain rosemary extract, which is designed to fend off insect pests. So, you may need to make your own food blend in order to test this on death feigning beetles. The naturally long lifespans of the blue death feigning beetle might be a combination of genetics and environment. It is still unlikely that they encounter

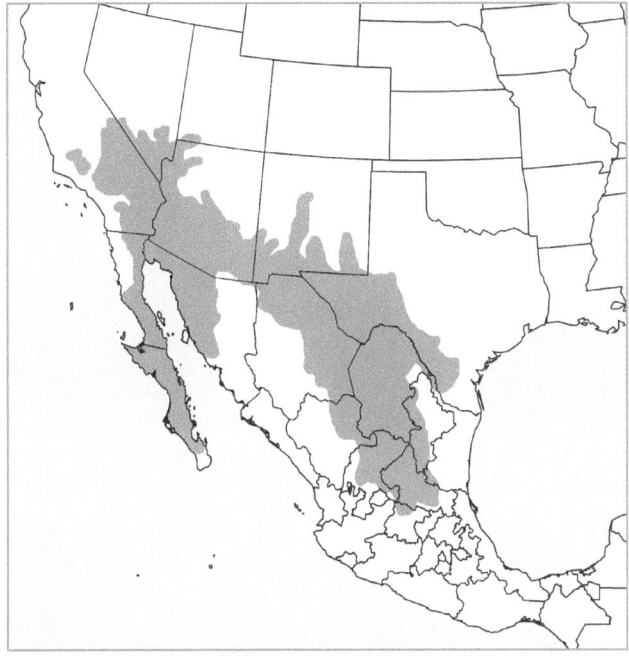

**Figure 6.26**
Distribution map of the creosote bush (*Larea tridentata*). This map closely matches the distribution map of death feigning beetles.

a diet of broccoli in their natural habitat. So, other than genetics, what might be going on in their natural diet?

There is one interesting possibility, and it is highly speculative. Antioxidants increase lifespans in invertebrates. One of the most powerful is a chemical called nordihydroguaiaretic acid (abbreviated NDGA). What is interesting is that NDGA can increase lifespan in fruit flies and nematodes as well as mice. More interesting than that is the fact that the leaves of creosote bush are high in NDGA. Why care? When you consider the distribution map of the creosote bush and compare it to that of death feigning beetles, they overlap significantly. It might be interesting to see if death feigning beetles would consume creosote bush leaves and whether this alters their lifespan. If the beetles seem uninterested in the leaves, there are other possibilities.

The beetles might normally consume dead insects that use the creosote bush as a host. Over one hundred different insects use creosote bushes as a food source. So, it could be possible that death feigning beetles are exposed to NDGA through consuming insects that feed on creosote bush. It might be a worthwhile experiment to feed other insects some NDGA and then feed those insects to death feigning beetles to see what happens.

## Incubators

The only thing an incubator must do is keep temperature. Everything else is for looks and ease of use. In its simplest form, an incubator can be a box containing an incandescent light bulb. It has to be of the appropriate wattage. A step up from that would be an insulated box with a heater that can be set to the desired temperature. You can find some videos online for building this type of do-it-yourself 5-minute incubator.

For many years, the least expensive incubators were for chicken eggs. They had a fixed temperature designed for chickens. These won't do for insects that need lower temperatures. Therefore, you need to look at the specifications of the incubator to find one that you can adjust to lower temperatures. Inexpensive chicken incubators are available that come with pre-set or factory-set values that are good for chicken eggs. Many can be re-programmed to work for insects.

The next parameter to check before buying is whether it will hold the rearing containers you plan to use. The tiny incubators are attractive for their price tag, but they are not usually very large. You can still find a decent incubator that will work that is not terribly expensive (an economy incubator). Sometimes low tech is more robust. Therefore, it might be advisable to stay as low tech as possible (not just for budgetary concerns).

Beyond this, there are incubators at all scales of size and price. You can buy incubators for reptiles, insects, microbes, plants and so on up to walk-in incubators with air filtration systems and built-in lab benches. You don't need that!

**Figure 6.27**
A new glass-door merchandiser (left) came from a salvage dealer at an extreme discount because it was missing its compressor unit. Unneeded parts in good condition were sold online, and copper was sold to a local recycler to recoup costs. An IncuKit XL was installed for temperature control. A programmable timer light switch was installed to regulate the lighting that was already a part of the cabinet doors. Both control units (top right) were installed where an advertising banner was located. The heating unit was mounted on the ceiling in place of the old circulating fan and hidden behind the original grid (middle right). The thermistor was mounted in place of the old one using a plastic test tube and a rubber mounting washer (bottom right). A glass dish containing saturated salt was placed in the bottom of the unit and a pump bottle with water was stored inside to be used for the larvae and pupae. Empty containers were kept inside to minimize the need for outside storage.

If you do decide to scale up and have a desire to possess a large incubator, there is some good news. One of the least expensive options is to convert a nonfunctional refrigerator, freezer or glass door merchandiser into an incubator. It is already an insulated box with shelves in it. You can also frequently find them for free on the curb or listed for free in online marketplaces.

The only thing needed is the ability to warm the box to the right temperature. A few companies sell incubator heater kits for cabinet-style incubators. These kits cost about the same as an economy chicken incubator. So, making the decision to scale up is less about cost than it is about other resources like space and your level of skill at building things.

Commonly available kits require some level of skill with power tools like a drill and possibly a saw. You can review installation manuals online before you decide to buy one. A drill is almost a necessity for running wires from the controller to the heater inside the cabinet. If you want to just run the wires where the door and the cabinet meet, you can do this if the wires are thin. If not, you may need to cut a notch in the magnetic gasket that seals the door closed. You may need a saw, depending on how you need to mount the heater and controller.

These kits require limited skill with electrical wiring to connect power to the controller. You normally do this with a wire nut. You will also have to connect a temperature sensor. It is about the same level of difficulty as installing a ceiling fan. For a lot of people, a DIY incubator of large size is easily achievable. If you feel a need to really scale up, it is common for hobbyists to convert a closet or bedroom into a warm space for their insects.

## Humidity

You can easily create a humid chamber at 75% relative humidity (RH). All you need is a large plastic box in which you place smaller containers - one for a salt solution and others for your bugs. The salt solution is saturated NaCl. You make it by filling the smaller box with salt pellets. The pellets are the kind used in water softeners. Then just add some water. Don't

**Figure 6.28**
Demonstration of a humidity chamber. In this small-scale example, two acrylic containers are housed inside a third sealed container. On the left is a small open acrylic box that contains the saturated salt (NaCl) solution which is just a few salt pellets for a water softener that were placed in a little bit of water. To the right is an open top housing setup for a single larva. Both containers are sealed inside a larger acrylic box. This should maintain the desired 75% RH. Larger air-tight totes can be used in a similar fashion to hold many small containers in a humid environment and the same type of system can be set up inside an incubator.

completely dissolve the salt pellets. Some of the pellets should remain setting in the solution like rocks. Some people also sprinkle a few grains of table salt into the bottom of the larger container. The idea is to reach equilibrium between the solid salt, air humidity and the saturated salt solution. Then put the lid onto the larger container to seal it all in. This is the old-school way to regulate humidity without electronic gadgets and expensive equipment. The same process is used to keep the humidity at a regulated level inside a growth chamber or incubator. You can use salts other than table salt to regulate different humidity levels. Commonly available salts like de-icer/ice melt (magnesium chloride; $MgCl_2$) can maintain ~26% RH. On the higher end, potassium chloride (KCl) provides ~80% RH. A 0-0-60 fertilizer (potassium nitrate; $KNO_3$) can maintain ~85% RH. The values will vary several percentage points depending upon the temperature.

### Sterilizing materials

In a research lab, you can sterilize substrate materials using an autoclave. In a home setting, you have two primary choices to eliminate microbes and pests: the oven and the freezer. Bleach is also a good choice for solid materials like containers. You can probably use bleach for pure sand with adequate rinsing. If neither of those seems appropriate, then rubbing alcohol and grain alcohol (either one at ~70%) are excellent alternatives for disinfection.

You can use dry heat for stored grains. Thirty minutes of exposure to 130°F (55°C) should kill insect pests like moth larvae. Similarly, heat (usually 65°C or 150°F) for as little as five minutes kills living organisms. You can put materials in hot water or hot moist air. Again, moist heat is your friend when it comes to eliminating most insects and microbes. You can do this for sand and coir mixes. You sift the sand-coir mix before baking it so that it is useful for egg collection. It is also more difficult to sift moist sand mixes than it is to sift dry sand mixes.

Do the sifting first and add enough water to make the mix capable of clumping. If you add too much water, then you have to wait a long time for the sand-coir mix to dry out. It will probably not completely dry while you bake it in the oven. You want to heat the mix up to a high enough temperature for a long enough time to kill microbes. The standard protocol mentions using several hours of baking. You can test if the substrate is getting hot enough by using a cooking thermometer. You should adjust your methods accordingly. Sterilizing your substrate mixes is something that is best done well in advance of when you need

**Figure 6.29**
Standard testing sieves (sifters) come with a label certifying their particle sizes (top). The one presented here is brass (middle row). Sifted substrate is moist enough when it can clump or hold its shape after being squeezed like that shown in the bottom panel.

them. It helps to make a batch of sterilized substrate, let it dry, and store it in a sealed container for later use.

You can sterilize other materials like organic mixes by freezing them. The presence of moisture is probably a beneficial thing to have. Freezing at normal freezer temperatures generates the formation of ice crystals. On a cellular level, ice crystals tend to have the effect of causing a lot of damage. So, the ice formation during freezing kills any bugs or microbes in the mix. It is conventional to freeze items for 48 hours. Freezing items to kill insect pests and microbes has been focused on soil ecology, food safety, or preserving museum specimens. We have only anecdotal evidence to support its use for insect rearing. Nonetheless, we do what we can to protect our beetles.

You will frequently need to clean and sterilize containers and other objects before they are re-used. Just be aware that sand is not good for appliances! A quick rinse of all your containers using a garden hose outdoors is a good idea. This is done to avoid ruining your plumbing and home appliances.

You can use bleach to sterilize containers and plastic aquarium decorations. Avoid bleaching yourself, your clothing and anything you do not want to destroy. Rubber gloves and goggles can be handy in this situation (also known as personal protective equipment). Avoid using bleach with metal containers and unsealed surfaces. Sufficient bleach is ⅓ cup per gallon of water. Submerge the items in the bleach solution for 20 minutes in a large plastic tub or in a bathtub. After the waiting period, rinse the containers and other objects with water. Then set them on a clean surface to dry.

A second method to get containers clean is to treat them like normal dishes. Run them through the dishwasher. You can wash "critter" cages and similar plastic items that are heat-resistant on the top dishwasher shelf.

Alcohol is a good sanitizer. Pure grain alcohol (200 proof ethanol) is somewhat expensive when purchased as a beverage. This is because of the taxes imposed. It works well at >60% concentration. One popular brand of pure grain drinking alcohol sold in the United States is available ready to use as a disinfectant at 151 proof (75.5%). Higher percentages and lower percentages are less effective at killing microbes. The same rules apply for isopropyl alcohol. This is also known as rubbing alcohol. It is available diluted to a 70% concentration. In addition to being disinfectants, both will function well at removing the ink used by most "permanent" markers. This comes in handy if you like to label your containers with permanent markers and then later want to wash them up, remove the markings, and use the containers again.

If you are in the process of bleaching containers and removing labels, it probably means that you are getting finished with a breeding season or perhaps gearing up for another one to start.

Sometimes it is helpful to wash the sand substrate and eliminate all the organic debris. Sifting the used dry sand to remove large debris can be helpful, but it is not necessary. The basic strategy is to first place the sand into the tub. Then use a garden hose to fill the tub with enough water to cover all the sand. Make sure you have a couple inches of water above the sand level. Stir the sand to make the coir and other low-density material get suspended for a short time in the water. The sand will settle. While the organics remain suspended, pour off the water. Do this by tilting the tub to the side at a shallow angle to get rid of the debris. Repeat the process until the sand and water are clean. This process is best done outdoors with a large plastic tub, but you can do it on a small scale indoors. The caveat is that sand that escapes into your sink drain is not great for your plumbing. At this point, you can bake the wet sand, if desired. You can also allow it to air dry and store it for future use.

### Section Summary

- We can identify the sexes by:
  - hairy male antennae = *Asbolus*, *Schizillus*? and some *Cryptoglossa* species
  - tubercles on male legs = certain *Cryptoglossa* species
  - egg laying in females
  - mounting behavior in males
- Some big choices have to be made
  - how much organic material and what type to use
  - how much clay to use
  - whether or not to stratify larvae
- We have to choose some essential ingredients too
  - food - what type and how much
  - water - to drink if needed and to keep substrates moist below the surface
  - temperature - heat lamps, pads or incubators depending on the life stages
  - humidity - maintained with salt solutions
  - keeping things clean - baking, freezing, bleach and alcohol

# 7. CAPTIVE BREEDING

## 7.1 The original '14 recipe

The captive breeding breakthrough that allowed blue death feigning beetles to be reared in captivity in 2014 got a lot of people excited online. The news generated a lot of questions too. Many people wondered if this was a fluke or if this was beyond most people's abilities. I actually waited almost two years to share my news because I wanted to make sure it was not an accident.

Even though the important parts were posted online, a lot of people just wanted a clear recipe. That original recipe for raising blue death feigning beetles is presented here. The most important goal at that time was to have something that was working and could be reproduced. It works for *A. verrucosus*, *A. mexicanus mexicanus*, *A. laevis* and *C. infausta* without any changes.

As you saw from the last section, many breeders have shared their insights on potential improvements. This recipe is not a fluke, and it is very much reproducible. Video proof from other breeders can be found on YouTube in the playlist of my channel @s_dean_rider_jr.

Consider this to be your starting recipe. From here you can try improvements like those listed in the previous chapter.

## 7.2 Standardized methods

### Standard substrate

Play sand is used for adults to lay eggs. "Standard substrate" is 1:1 sand to coir mix (by volume) with a moisture gradient for larvae and pupae. First, pass dry materials through a standard number 20 sieve. Before baking, substrates should be moistened to the point where the material can form clumps. This is then heat treated at 250°F (121°C) in an oven for several hours. Glass, aluminum and stainless steel pans work for this purpose. Cooled, dried substrate is ready for use. Maintain substrate moisture gradients by bottom watering the substrate using a straw. Bury the straw vertically. The straw should extend to the top and to the bottom of the housing container you choose to use.

### Standard diet

Use fresh organic carrots and dried crickets for all feeding stages. Once or twice weekly, remove and replace the food if it became desiccated (carrots) or moldy (crickets).

### Standard temperature

Use 72-75°F (22-24°C) for eggs, first instars and hardened adults. Use 80-88°F (27-31°C) for older larvae, pupae and young beetles. Stay on the lower range for *A. mexicanus*. Use 80°F (27°C) for hardening of teneral adults. Use an incubator to maintain elevated temperatures.

### Standard relative humidity (RH)

Use 40% and up for hardened adults. Use 75% for other stages. Maintain a relative humidity of 75% using saturated salt solutions housed inside closed incubators or housing spaces where you have your rearing containers.

## 7.3 Detailed instructions

### Eggs

Allow a mixed population of adults to randomly breed at 72-76°F (22-24°C) in a 10 gallon tank (38.7 liters) or relatively large container with lots of surface area and play sand that is 3-4 inches deep (10 cm). A moisture gradient and a buried carrot may further stimulate egg laying. Egg laying will probably be dependent on photoperiod, temperature, and availability of food. Provide plenty of fresh organic carrots and dried crickets to adults. Sift sand on a weekly basis using a standard #16 or #20 sieve to obtain eggs of similar age. Maintain eggs on sand at 72-76°F (22-24°C) and 75-

80 percent RH. Larvae will hatch from viable eggs in about two to three weeks. Discard eggs that are four weeks old or older.

### First instar larvae

First instars probably do not feed. Transfer similarly aged larvae to group housing. Individuals can be moved to single housing as desired within a few days of hatching. For group housing, higher ratios of coir (more than 10%) are more likely to produce better survival. Place larvae into a 1:1 sand to coir mix with a moisture gradient and allow them to hang out. At about one week of age at 72-76°F (22-24°C) and 40-75% RH, they will molt to the second instar. Higher temperatures at this stage appear to be detrimental to survival.

### 2nd to 5th instar larvae

This is an early growth phase for larvae. Place larvae into a 1:1 sand to coir mix with a moisture gradient and allow them to hang out at 72-76°F (22-24°C) and 75% RH. Individuals maintained in containers without substrate but with 75% RH survived several weeks. The substrate and moisture gradient may not be necessary, but larvae seemed unhappy, so they were returned to containers with substrate. Feed larvae dried crickets and fresh carrots. They will molt and grow. Head capsules can be measured to determine approximate instar, if desired. Head capsules should reach about 1.2 mm between 3 and 6 weeks of age, indicating 3rd instar. By ten (10) weeks of age, head capsules should be 2 mm, indicating 5th instar. Move larvae into higher temperatures for potentially faster growth. The best time to move them to higher temperatures seems to be between 50 and 100 days of age. Higher temperatures are between 80-95°F (30-35°C).

### Maturing larvae (instars 5-9+)

Larvae at this stage should be housed individually. It seems to be important to get maturing larvae into higher temperatures (but not too high) well before they reach the wandering stage to induce them to pupate early and without aestivation. Pupation has not been observed at temperatures below 86°F (30°C) or above 95°F (35°C). Fifteen weeks (100 days) is the optimal time to make the shift from 75°F (24°C) to about 88-90°F (31-32°C) and 75% RH. Transferring larvae at a younger age actually results in an overall longer time to adult formation. Waiting beyond 100 days needlessly delays further development. Feed them carrots and dried crickets and watch for wandering behavior or reduced feeding. Mature larvae will wander, looking for a suitable location where they can pupate in isolation. At this stage, the depth of the substrate may be important, mostly for maintaining moisture in the substrate without having it become too labor-intensive. The standard substrate should be about 4-5 inches deep with a moisture gradient. Larvae will create a pupal cell deep in the substrate, often at the very bottom of the container. No one knows the exact trigger for pupation, but if you disturb mature larvae inside pupal cells, it will certainly delay pupation. Maintain the moisture gradient and try not to disturb them once they make a pupal cell. It can take 5-10 weeks to see pupae form at this temperature.

### Pupae

Maintain moisture gradients, temperature (88°F/31°C) and relative humidity (75%). Try not to disturb them too much. After about two weeks (10-16 days), they will eclose and become beetles.

### Young beetles

Allow newly eclosed beetles to remain in their pupal cell for at least 5 days. Watch for legs to turn black and for beetles to right themselves. You can remove them from their pupal cell if they darken and have already turned themselves over. Most beetles are probably capable of digging their way out. Some will not and can die if not removed from the substrate. Dig them up on day 7 post-eclosion if you have concerns about them being unable to dig themselves out. Move them to lower temperatures and high humidity (75-80°F/24-26°C, and 75% RH) for about a month. Keep them on a plain sand substrate at this point and offer them carrots and crickets. Do not induce death feigning at this stage because it can be lethal to the rather delicate beetles. The adults have a teneral phase that lasts several weeks. During this time, they will turn from rust-colored to black, and produce the blue waxy covering. The wax will begin before the black color has completed. Adults that have emerged from a pupal cell will frequently display head standing behavior. This is generally a good sign. Watch for color changes, and for feeding behavior. After about a month under these conditions, and if the beetles are eating well, they can generally be transferred to normal room temperatures and humidity. Make sure they have access to food and a source of water (fresh carrots, dried crickets, & a watering vial) because desiccation is still a possibility.

### Environmentally hardened beetles

Enjoy, and try to get another generation…

---

**Section Summary**
- Let adult beetles breed and make eggs
- Keep larvae in a moisture gradient and well fed
- Move 100-day-old larvae to 88°F to induce pupation
- Don't disturb mature larvae, pupae and teneral adults
- Move teneral adults to display tanks when they mature

---

# 8. CITIZEN SCIENCE

Citizen science is just as useful as the science done in research labs at universities and companies. In all cases, what is at stake is the reputation of the person or the institution doing the work. Stay dedicated to your craft. If you have something useful to share, there is a place for the information and the specimens you

|  | Egg | 1st instar larva | Mature larva | Pupa | Teneral adult |
|---|---|---|---|---|---|
| A. laevis | research | research | reported | reported | reported |
| A. mexicanus | research | research | research | research | reported |
| A. papillosus | x | x | x | x | x |
| A. verrucosus | research | research | research | research | research |
| C. asperata | x | x | x | x | x |
| C. bicostata | x | x | x | x | x |
| C. caraboides | x | x | x | x | x |
| C. infausta | research | research | research | reported | reported |
| C. michelbacheri | x | x | x | x | x |
| C. muricata | research | research | research | reported | reported |
| C. seriata | x | x | x | x | x |
| C. spiculifera | research | x | x | x | x |
| C. variolosa | reported | reported | research | x | x |
| S. laticeps | x | x | research | x | x |
| S. nunenmacheri | research | research | research | research | x |

### Figure 8.1

A report card of sorts, showing where there are gaps in scientific knowledge for the morphology of immature death feigning beetle species. A green box with the word research means that research has been published on these stages. Reports mean someone has mentioned or shown examples outside of a scientific publication but formal research has not been done. An "x" means the stage has not been reported. Five of the six species for which no immature stages are known are exclusive to Mexico.

generate. Behavioral studies are almost unheard of. This represents a wide field of opportunity. The text presented here shows a few areas where there are obvious gaps in our knowledge of death feigning beetles. No doubt there are many ideas that have not been covered.

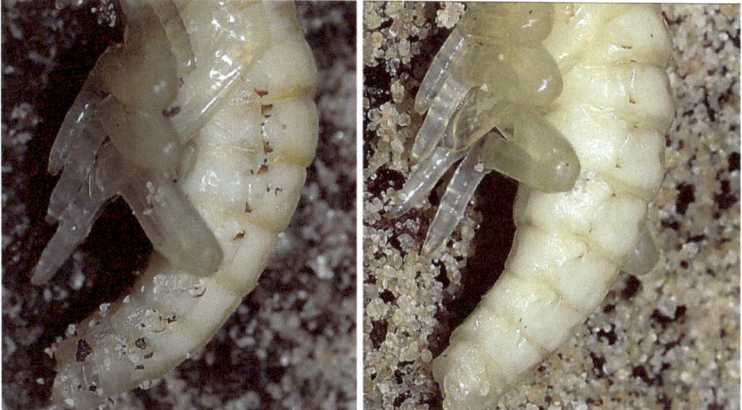

**Figure 8.2**
Comparative morphology is needed. These two pupae may look the same at first glance, but the one on the left (*Asbolus verrucosus*) has more darkened points and "gin traps" on the last few abdominal segments than the one on the right where the protrusions are reduced to fleshy lobes (*Asbolus mexicanus mexicanus*). These kinds of differences can only be found if pupae are available for study.

## Improved rearing

It should be clear that we are making progress. Methods to captively breed death feigning beetles as pets are improving. The extreme efforts of many hobbyists have been fruitful. We can now breed at least five species in captivity. However, these efforts have not led to large-scale availability of captive bred beetles for the pet trade. Therefore, we need improved concepts and methods. The bug-loving community struggles to improve captive breeding. It helps everyone if you share any good tips and tricks. This will move captive breeding forward. You should share your insights in online forums dedicated to invertebrates. These places are where others will likely have their own experiences to share.

## Missing life stages

The lack of good protocols for captive breeding leads to other deficiencies. For example, the immature stages of many death

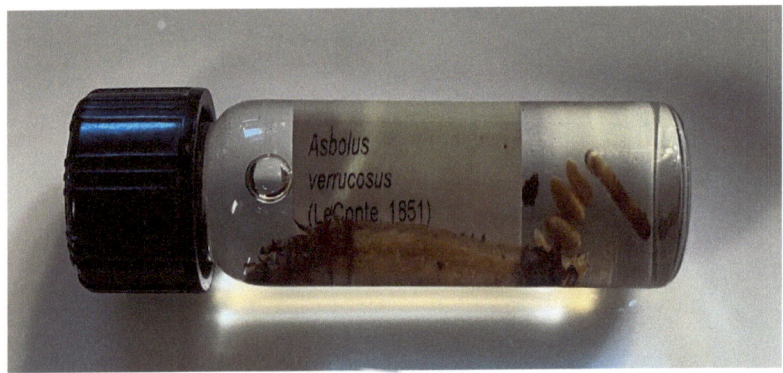

**Figure 8.3**

Alcohol preserved specimens of eggs and larvae for the blue death feigning beetle *Asbolus verrucosus*.

feigning beetles have never been described by scientists. These missing life stages prevent the scientific community from having a complete picture. We can still improve knowledge on the biology and taxonomy of these beetle species. The eggs, first instar larvae, mature larvae and pupae are needed for many species. You can deposit them into a museum or voucher location. There are many across the country. Taxonomists could eventually use them. This will help complete the picture of what these insects look like and how they differ from one another. We should note that much of the information that is missing is for Mexican species.

You can find specimen deposit locations at land-grant (agriculture) universities. Many have large research insect collections. An easy way to find them is by an online search for "voucher insect specimen deposit" and the state you live in. The most common way to preserve immature beetle stages is with alcohol. Place them into 70% alcohol and seal them in a vial. Print labels with a laser printer (not laser jet) to prevent dissolving the ink in alcohol. You can place such labels inside the alcohol with the specimens. The institution that accepts voucher specimens will probably require additional information. They will guide you on what to include on labels or if they have special labels they want used. It helps the scientific community to have more than one specimen to examine. If a person is able to generate 5-10 specimens for any missing life stage, that would be a huge advancement.

## Lifespan studies

We like to have long-lived beetles. We also want to know how long we can expect a beetle species to live. Fastidious record keepers should consider tracking how long individual beetles live. It would be wonderful to have this information for all species of death feigning beetles. So, if you happen to acquire some beetles, note the starting date as well as when each of them dies. This can add to the greater body of knowledge that we have on a given species. Even if ten different people each had one beetle, the combined data would be worthwhile. We lack this type of information for even common pet species like *C. muricata* and *C. variolosa*. Thus, there is plenty of opportunity to provide new insight on these popular beetles.

## Behavioral studies

The majority of the research that has been focused on these beetles has been on morphology and taxonomy. However, insects display interesting behaviors. Without being able to raise large numbers of specimens in captivity, it is difficult to observe and test their behavior. This is especially true for immature stages of death feigning beetles. For example, since they are death feigning beetles, do all of them have larvae that play dead? How long do they stay catatonic? Do larvae other than the blue death feigning beetle bleed when they play dead? In this area, we already have some established methods like the "hand transfer method" and the "rotisserie method". These are used for inducing death feigning in larvae to see how these insects behave. Videos are available at https://zenodo.org/records/5813945. But, what about things no one has ever noticed or studied? How about food choice tests? There are so many things that have never been documented in the behavior arena. It seems like there are great opportunities for some citizen science!

## Population studies

It is normal for populations to differ based on their location even though they are the same species. Often, these differences are revealed by comparing populations from different latitudes or altitudes. The geographic regions where death feigning beetles live can cover tens of thousands of square kilometers. This certainly is the case for *A. verrucosus*, *A. mexicanus*, *C. muricata*, *C. infausta*, and *C. variolosa*. *Schizillus* species and *A. mexicanus* have isolated populations in distant locations. Some people report being able to get *A. verrucosus* to complete their life cycle without a temperature spike. This seems unusual. The origin of the founding population might be responsible. You may find it interesting to test samples of beetles from distant locations. They may show differences in their behaviors and requirements for completing their life cycle.

## Where do they hide?

April is peak season for finding these beetles in their natural habitats. By mid October in the Mojave and Sonoran deserts, they are very difficult to find. We know they have long lifespans that last years, so the big question is: where do they go in winter? This could be a really worthwhile thing to find out.

---

### Section Summary
- There are many things we do not know about death feigning beetles.
- Most of the things we are missing are not difficult to figure out.
- It is time for more citizen science!

## 9. EPILOGUE

When I started this book, I had no plans to visit the desert. However, inclement weather stepped in during a road trip. The trip veered south from the Grand Canyon. Before the trip was finished, I would run barefoot through the Mojave Desert and make sand angels in the Devil's Playground. I also got to hike rocky slopes in the Sonoran Desert. This allowed me to photograph the habitats, plants, soil and some insects that eventually appeared in this book. Along the way, I was able to walk the desert at night and find tenebrionids congregating near ant hills.

If you also find yourself able to tour the desert, this book should help you find and identify death feigning beetles. We started by defining the characteristics that make beetles unique. Then we examined some important characteristics of darkling beetles. Namely, we looked at the lack of a notopleural suture, the tarsal formula and the appearance of the antennae. We identify death feigning beetles and their relatives by their inability to produce chemical defenses. When we looked at the death feigning beetle species, only six characters were important. The eyes, antennae, pronotum, tarsal setae, elytra and the prosternal process are enough to distinguish each species. Therefore, identifying individual species becomes fairly straight-forward.

We then looked at keeping beetles as pets. The chapter on keeping beetles is not too complex because we can care for these beetles with minimal effort. They can eat a wide variety of foods and need some moisture to survive. You can keep them in just about any smooth walled container, and you don't have to worry about them escaping. They do appreciate warmth, but normal household temperatures are fine for them. Regrettably, we cannot prevent or cure any of the parasites and diseases of these beetles.

If you plan to keep these beetles as pets, there is more than enough information here to get you started and to keep you experimenting for years to come. When we think of breeding beetles in captivity, we look to the environment. We want to know what beetles might need to reproduce optimally. The best chance we have to breed beetles is to understand the ingredients we see in the natural environment. Chapter 6 is a description of the possible ingredients. We learn what the ingredients do. Chapter 7 is where we get a basic recipe. It tells us how much of each ingredient to use, what temperature to use, and how long to wait. The recipe works, but can use a bit of refinement. Our job is to experiment with different substrate mixes, temperatures and timing to get better results. Better captive breeding will no doubt lead to an improved pet industry and open more doors to scientific research.

I encourage you to visit online resources such as arachnoboards.com or the beetleforum.net to see other peoples' viewpoints on rearing beetles. You can also share your beetle experiences there. Rus Wilson has produced a multi-part YouTube video series on blue death feigning beetle breeding. It is presented on the Aquarimax Pets channel. So, there are a number of resources available to help you, in addition to this book.

Death feigning beetles are among the larger and more impressive insects available in North America. We have delved into some rarely thought about aspects of finding, keeping and breeding death feigning beetles. There is no other resource available that goes into the depth that this book does for the sake of these beloved creatures. I hope it will serve as a reference that you can return to repeatedly.

## 10. RESOURCES

This list was made for those individuals who want to copy what was done for rearing setups and experiments presented in this book. It is also here for anyone who might wonder what specific items were used and where they came from.

### Beetle Sources

Beetles have come from the following sources:
**Bugs In Cyberspace**
  https://bugsincyberspace.com

**Invertebrate Dude**
  https://www.invertebratedude.com/

**The Spider Room**
  https://thespiderroom.com

**Bug Cage Company**
  https://bugcagecompany.com/

### Substrate Mixes

The Asbolus Substrate that was tested was from:
**US Invertebrate LLC**
  https://usinvertebratellc.com/

The calcium bentonite clay that was tested was from:
**Mojave Pure**
  https://www.mojavepure.com/

## Containers

Plastic containers mostly came from:
**United States Plastic Corp.**
    **Item 70469 12 oz. Clear PET Square Beverage Bottle**
    **Item 55372 Clear Plastic Box with Removable Lid 2-5/16" L x 2-5/16" W x 6-3/16" Hgt.**
    https://www.usplastic.com/

The clear boxes were also available from:
**AMAC Plastic Products Corp**
    **Item 102C Box in their Packaging M series**
    https://www.amac1960.com/collections/m-series-packaging

## Incubator Kits

The incubator kit used was the IncuKit XL from:
**Incubator Warehouse**
    https://incubatorwarehouse.com/collections/egg-incubator-accessories-incukits

## Large Incubators

You can look for free stuff and great deals at the sites below and search for "merchandiser", "fridge", "freezer" for conversions or directly search for an "incubator"...

**Craigslist:** craigslist.org    **GovDeals:** govdeals.com
**eBay:** ebay.com

Also, many local universities usually have surplus items that include incubators and glass door fridges.

## Aquariums

The 2.5 gallon aquariums and metal covers were from:
**Aquaeon**
   https://www.aqueon.com/products/aquariums/standard-glass-rectangle-aquariums
   **The aquariums are typically sold in pet stores and the website might direct you to a local store for purchases.**

**WaterKingdom (eBay store)**
   Lee's Aquarium Metallic Screen Top for 2.5G
   https://www.ebay.com/str/waterkingdom
   **These don't appear to be available anywhere else online but were popular many years ago. Metal screen lids also work to support heat lamps. The one listed here has a locking mechanism and is low profile.**

## Heatlamps

Heatlamps and domes were from:
**Zoo Med Laboratories Inc.**
   **Creatures Dome Lamp Fixture, 40 Watt**
   **Nano Ceramic Heat Emitter, 40 Watt**
   https://zoomed.com/

## Tiny plants

Micro cacti used in the tequila bottle display were from:
**Tierra Sol Studio**
   https://tierrasolstudio.com/

## Miscellaneous items

Most other supplies were purchased at local pet stores, hardware stores and food service stores or through one of the large online retailers. This included soufflé cups, conical bottomed test tubes, straws, sand, plaster, coir, critter cages, salt pellets, crickets, carrots, kibble, vials, paint brushes, insect pins, alcohol, and more. INSTA-DRI nail polish and Titebond III Ultimate Wood Glue were used to decorate beetles.

## Useful terms

Selected from a manuscript originally prepared by
John B. Smith, Sc.d. in 1906
now in the public domain

**Abdomen**: the third or posterior division of the insect body: consists normally of nine or ten apparent segments, but actual number is a mooted question: bears no functional legs in the adult stage.

**Adult**: the stage when an insect is sexually mature and ready to reproduce normally.

**Aestivation**: applied to summer dormancy.

**Antenna -ae**: two jointed, sensory organs, borne, one on each side of the head, commonly termed horns or feelers.

**Anterior**: in front; before; in Dip., that face of the leg which is visible from the front when the leg is laterally extended and bristles on that face are anterior.

**Anus**: the end of the digestive tract, through which the food remnants are passed: the posterior part of the individual: specifically, in Coccidae, a more or less circular opening on the dorsal surface of the pygidium, varying in location as regards the circumgenital gland orifices: = anal orifice.

**Apical**: at, near or pertaining to the apex; usually of a wing.

**Apterous**: without wings.

**Arid**: Applied to regions in which the normal rainfall is insufficient to produce ordinary farm crops without irrigation, and in which desert conditions prevail: see humid.
**Arthropods**: all those articulates having jointed legs.
**Back**: the dorsum or upper surface.
**Bi**: prefix, means two.
**Bristle**: a stiff hair, usually short and blunt.
**Carina -ae**: an elevated ridge or keel, not necessarily high or acute. Carinate: a surface having carinae.
**Carnivorous**: a feeder upon flesh food.
**Caterpillar**: the term applied to the larvae of Lepidoptera.
**Cavity -as**: a hollow space or opening.
**Centimeter**: abb. cm.: = 0.01 meter = 0.394 inch; 2.54 cm. = one inch.
**Chrysalis or -id**: applied specifically to the intermedial stage between larva and adult in butterflies: see pupa.
**Claws**: the claw or hook-like structures at the end of the foot or tarsus.
**Coarctate**: contracted: compacted: applied to that form of pupa in which all the members of the future adult are concealed by a thickened, usually cylindric case or covering, which is often the hardened skin of the larva: beginning with a narrow base, then dilated and thickened.
**Coleoptera**: sheath-winged: an order with the primaries coriaceous, used as a cover only, meeting in a straight line dorsally; mouth mandibulate; pro-thorax free; transformation complete: the beetles: the term has also been applied to the two elytra together.
**Concave**: hollowed out; the interior of a sphere as opposed to the outer or convex surface: concave veins are those that occupy the bottoms of troughs or grooves on the upper surface of a wing; see convex veins.
**Conspicuous**: striking: easily seen at a glance.
**Convex**: the outer curved surface of a segment of a sphere; opposed to concave: convex veins are those which occupy the

summits of ridges on the upper surface of - wing; see concave veins.

**Copulate**: to unite in sexual intercourse.

**Corvinus**: crow-black; deep, shining black with a greenish lustre.

**Costa**: any elevated ridge that is rounded at its crest: the thickened anterior margin of any wing, but usually the primaries: in Comstock, the vein extending along the anterior margin of the wing from base to the point of junction with subcosta.

**Costate**: ribbed; marked with elevated thickened lines.

**Coxa -ae**: the basal segment of the leg, by means of which it is articulated to the body.

**Coxal cavity**: the opening or space in which the Coxa articulates; in Coleoptera the cavity is open when the epimera do not extend to the sternum; closed or entire when the epimera reach the sternum or join medially as in Rhynchophora; the cavities are separated when the prosternum extends between them, confluent when it does not: see acetabulum.

**Crepuscular**: active or flying at dusk or dawn.

**Crypto**: hidden, concealed.

**Dash**: a short disconnected streak or mark.

**Dense**: thickly crowded together.

**Dentate**: toothed: with acute teeth, the sides of which are equal and the tip is above the middle of base.

**Di**: as a prefix, = two.

**Dimorphism**: a difference in form, color, etc, between individuals of the same species, characterizing two distinct types: may be seasonal, sexual or geographic.

**Distal**: that part of a joint farthest from the body.

**Diurnal**: such insects as are active or habitually fly by day only.

**Divergent**: spreading out from a common base; in Coleoptera, tarsal claws are divergent when they spread out only a little; divaricate when they separate widely.

**Dominant**: a character more constant and conspicuous than any other: a type or series occurring in large numbers both as to genera, species and individuals and in which differentiation is yet active.

**Dorsal**: of or belonging to the upper surface: in Diptera, that face of the laterally extended legs visible from above.

**Ecdysis**: the process of casting the skin; moulting.

**Egg**: a simple cell, capable of fertilization, containing the germ, the food-yolk necessary for its nutriment, and a covering membrane: a single ovum or cell from an ovary: the first stage of the insect.

**Egg-burster**: a projecting point on the head or other part of an embryo, used in breaking the shell when hatching.

**Elytra**: the anterior leathery or chitinous wings of beetles, serving as coverings to the secondaries, commonly meeting in a straight line down the middle of dorsum in repose: also applied to the tegmina in Orthoptera.

**Elytron**: singular of elytra; q.v.

**Embryo**: the young animal before leaving the body of the parent or before emerging from the egg.

**Entomogenous**: growing in or on an insect: e.g. fungi.

**Entomography**: the description of an insect or of its life history.

**Entomology**: that branch of Zoology that deals with insects and, specifically, the Hexapods.

**Entomophagous**: feeding upon insects: specifically applied to those wasps that feed their young with larvae, etc.

**Evagination**: an extrusion formed by eversion or turning inside out.

**Exarate -us**: sulcated: sculptured.

**Excision**: with a deep cut: a notch or other cut-out part.

**Excretory**: those structures concerned in ridding the body of waste products.

**Exuvia -iae -ium**: the cast skin of a larval insect: in Diaspinae the larval skin when cast and incorporated in the scale.

**Eyes**: the organs of sight, composed of numerous facets, situated, one on each side of the head: the term is properly applied to compound eyes only but is sometimes used to designate also the simple eyes or ocelli.

**Facet**: a small face or surface: one of the parts, areas or lens-like divisions of the compound eye.

**Family**: a division of classification including a number of genera agreeing in one or a set of characters and so closely related that they are apparently descended from one stem: opinionative and indicated by the termination idae.

**Fecula**: the excrement of insects.

**Feeler**: commonly applied to antennae; q.v.

**Feelers**: tactile organs: the term is usually applied to the antennae but sometimes to the palpi, as mouth-feelers.

**Feet**: the legs or organs of locomotion; one pair attached to each thoracic segment; composed of coxa, trochanter, femur, tibia and tarsus only; plural of foot; q.v.

**Female**: that sex in which the ova are developed.

**Femoro-tibial**: pertaining to both femur and tibia or to the articulation between them.

**Femur -ora**: the thigh: usually the stoutest segment of the leg, articulated to the body through trochanter and coxa and bearing the tibia at its distal end: in Coccidae and quite commonly, the femur and trochanter are considered as one, for measuring purposes.

**Ferrugineous -ous, -eus, -osus**: rusty red-brown [Dragon's blood, but brighter].

**Filiform**: thread-like: slender and of equal diameter.

**Foot**: the tarsus, q.v.; improperly used to = leg; but in the plural form refers to legs rather than tarsi: see feet.

**Free**: unrestricted in movement: not firmly joined with or united to any other part: said of pupae when all the parts and appendages are separately encased as in Coleopteran.

**Fused**: run together: applied when two normally separated markings become confluent and have a common outline.

**Generation**: used as the equivalent of brood; q.v.

**Genus**: an assemblage of species agreeing in some one character or series of characters; usually considered as arbitrary and opinionative, though some consider it a natural assemblage.

**Glaber-rous**: smooth; free from all vestiture.

**Gland**: a cellular sac which separates or secretes from the blood specific portions to produce characteristic products - e.g. wax, saliva, silk, etc.

**Globose**: formed like a globe or sphere.

**Glossa**: the inner lobe of second maxilla, corresponding to the lacing of first maxilla: loosely used as a synonym for tongue: especially applied to the coiled structure of the Lepidoptera; see also ligula.

**Gregarious**: living in societies or communities; but not social.

**Grub**: an insect larva: a term loosely applied, but more specifically to larvae of Coleopteran and Hymenoptera.

**Habit -us**: the port or aspect: used to express a resemblance in general appearance.

**Habitat**; abbreviated Hab.: the region or place which an insect inhabits or where it was taken.

**Haemolymph**: the watery blood or lymph-like nutritive fluid of the lower invertebrates.

**Hair**: a slender, flexible filament of equal diameter.

**Hairy**: covered or clothed with hair.

**Head**: the first or anterior region of the insect body, articulated at its base to the thorax, bearing the mouth structures and antennae. It is now believed to be made up of seven primitive segments, named in order: 1, the ocular or protocerebral; 2, the antenna or deutocerebral; 3, second antenna or tritocerebral; 4, mandibular; 5, superlingual; 6, maxillary; 7, labial or 2d maxillary.

**Hexapoda**: tracheate arthropods with head, thorax and abdomen distinct, and only six legs in the adult stage: the true insects.

**Hips**: the coxa; q.v.

**Hirsute**: clothed with long, strong hair; shaggy.

**Holometabolous**: having a complete transformation; with egg, larval, pupal and adult stages distinctly separated.

**Host**: the individual infested by or upon which a parasite grows: also applied to the maker of a cell or other structure in which guest flies or other insects take up their abode.

**Humid**: applied to regions in which the normal rainfall is sufficient to produce ordinary farm crops without irrigation: see arid.
**Imago**: the adult or sexually developed insect.
**Inch**: the English and American standard of length in insect measurement: it is = 12 lines and = 25.4 mm.: usually expressed in units and hundredths, as 1.01.
**Inconspicuous**: not attracting attention or quickly noticeable.
**Inflated**: blown up; distended bladder-like.
**Insect**: a member of the class Insecta strictly limited.
**Insecta**: broadly defined, contains all articulates that are also tracheates and have the head free from the thorax; more strictly limited to those forms that have only three pairs of thoracic legs in the adult stage and a limited number of segments.
**Insectary**: a place or building where insects are bred and studied.
**Insectivorous**: feeding upon or devouring insects.
**Instar**: the period or stage between molts in the larva, numbered to designate the various periods; e.g. the first instar is the stage between the egg and first molt, etc.: see stadium.
**Intercostal**: between veins or costae; usually in the narrow grooves between veins in the costal region of a wing.
**Interocular**: between the eyes.
**Interspace**: Coleopteran; the plane surface between elytral striae: Lepidoptera spaces between wing veins not included in closed cells.
**Interstitial line**: the elevated ridge between two striae or series of punctures.
**Interval**: the space or time between two structures, sculptures or periods of development.
**Joint**: a segment or part between two incisures: an articulation.
**Knee**: the point of junction of femur and tibia.
**Labial**: referring, pertaining or belonging to the labium.
**Labial segment**: the $7^{th}$ segment of head = second maxillary segment.
**Labial suture**: is between labium and mentum.

**Labium**: the lower lip: a compound structure which forms the floor of the mouth in mandibulate insects, behind the first maxilla and opposed to the labium; formed by a fusion in embryonic life of separate right and left maxilla-like halves: in some of its developments referred to as the tongue.

**Labral suture**: is between labrum and clypeus.

**Labrum**: the upper lip; covers the base of the mandible and forms the roof of the mouth.

**Laevis -igatus**: smooth, shining and without elevations: said of a surface.

**Larva**: the second stage of insect development; comes from the egg or ovum, grows, and according to its kind, changes to a pupa or chrysalis or to an imago; bears various names in the different orders: see nymph; caterpillar slug; maggot; grub.

**Larvule**: applied to early stages of Ephemerid larvae when they appear to have no developed respiratory, circulatory or nervous systems.

**Lateral**: relating, pertaining or attached to the side.

**Latus**: the side: broad.

**Leg -s**: the jointed appendages attached to the thoracic segments, used in walking: the organs of locomotion other than wings: unjointed organs of locomotion are pro-legs or false legs; q.v.

**Lethargic**: torpid or inactive.

**Ligula**: the central sclerite of the labium, borne upon the mentum, usually single, sometimes paired: often used as synonymous with "glossa" and "tongue": corresponds to the united laciniae of right and left maxillae:

**Maggot**: applied to the footless larvae of Diptera.

**Male**: that sex having organs for the production of spermatozoa

**Medial**: referring to, or at the middle.

**Mental suture**: in Coleoptera, the line between mentum and gula.

**Mesal**: pertaining to, situated on or in the median plane of the body.

**Meso**: middle: as prefix, drops the o when stem begins with a vowel.

**Mesonotum**: the primitively upper surface of the 2d or middle thoracic ring.

**Mesosternal epimera**: in Coleoptera; the narrow pieces separating the meta-sternal from the meta-sternal episterna.

**Mesosternal episterna**: Coleoptera; on each side of mesosternum between anterior border and epimera; generally separated by a distinct suture.

**Mesotarsus**: the tarsus of the middle leg.

**Mesothoracotheca**: the pupal covering of the meso-thorax.

**Mesothorax**: the second or middle thoracic ring; bears the middle legs and the anterior wings.

**Mesotergum**: = mesonotum; q.v.

**Meta-**: posterior: used as a prefix to designate the third thoracic ring and its parts.

**Metamorphosis**: is that series of changes through which an insect passes in its growth from egg through larva and pupa to adult: it is complete when the pupa is inactive and does not feed; incomplete when there is no pupa or when the pupa is active and feeds.

**Metanotum**: the primitively upper surface of the third or posterior thoracic ring: in Diptera, the oval arched portion behind, beneath the scutellum best developed in flies with long, slender abdomen: e.g. Tipulidae.

**Metasternal**: relating or attached to the metasternum.

**Metathorax**: the third thoracic ring or segment; bears the hind legs and second pair of wings; variably distinct; sometimes closely united with the mesothorax and sometimes appearing as a portion of the abdomen.

**Meter**: the standard of length in the metric system = 39.37 inches: see centimeter and millimeter.

**Millimeter**: abb. mm.: 0.001 meter = 0.039 of an inch: roughly 25 mm. are counted to an inch in measuring insects.

**Mimetic**: when a species mimics or resembles another or some other object in appearance; but not in structure and other characters.

**Mimicry**: strictly, the resemblance of one animal to another not closely related animal, living in the same locality; often loosely used to denote also resemblance to plants and inanimate objects: Batesian mimicry is where one of two similar species is distasteful (so-called model), the other not distasteful (so-called mimic); Müllerian mimicry is where both species are distasteful.
**Moniliform**: beaded like a necklace.
**Moult**: a period in the transformation when the larva changes from one instar to another: the cast skin of a larva that has moulted.
**Mouth**: the anterior opening into the alimentary canal, where the feeding structures are situated and in which the food is prepared for ingestion.
**Mouthparts**: a collective name including labrum, mandibles, maxillae, labium and appendages = trophi.
**Muricate -us**: armed with sharp, rigid points.
**Nocturnal**: species that fly or are active at night.
**Notched**: indented, cut or nicked; usually a margin.
**Notopleural suture**: = dorso-pleural suture; q.v.
**Notum**: the dorsal or upper part of a segment: = tergum.
**Nude -us**: naked: a surface devoid of hair, scales or other vestiture.
**Nymph**: the larval stage of insects with incomplete metamorphosis: applies also to their pupal stage, and sometimes used as = pupa.
**Oblong**: longer than broad.
**Obtect**: wrapped in a hard covering.
**Obtected**: applied to pupae when they are covered with a chitinous case which confines and conceals all appendages, though their outlines may be marked on the surface: see free, and coarctate.
**Ommateum**: the compound eye.
**Ommatidium -ia**: one of the elements of which the compound eye is composed.
**Ontogeny**: the development of the individual as distinguished from that of the species: see phylogeny.

**Oögenesis**: the process of egg-formation.

**Order**: one of the primary divisions of the Class Insecta, based largely on wing structure and then usually ending in -ptera.

**Ovipositor**: the tubular or valved structure by means of which the eggs are placed; usually concealed; but sometimes extended far beyond the end of the body.

**Palpus**: a mouth feeler: tactile, usually jointed structures borne by the maxillae (maxillary palpi) and labium (labial palpi).

**Papilla**: a minute, soft projection: specifically the modified ligula in silk spinning caterpillars.

**Papillose** -us: pimply; a surface covered with raised dots or pimples.

**Parasite**: a species that lives in or on another animal or insect, and depends upon the tissue of the host for its food supply.

**Parasitic**: living on or in some other animal or insect in such a way as to derive all nourishment from the tissues of the host.

**Pectoralis**: relating to the breast.

**Pectoral plate**: in Coleoptera, the sternum.

**Phylogenetic**: relating to tribal or stem development.

**Phylogeny**: the development of a genus, family, tribe or class: see ontogeny.

**Phytophagus**: feeding upon plants.

**Pleura**: plural of pleuron or pleurum: the lateral sclerites between the dorsal and sternal portion of the thorax: in general, the sides of the body between the dorsum and sternum.

**Pleurites**: the sclerites into which the pleurum is divided.

**Pleuron**: the side of the thorax.

**Polyphagous**: eating many kinds of food.

**Posterior**: hinder or hindmost: opposed to anterior: in Diptera; applied to that face of the legs which is not visible when viewed from the front, the legs being laterally extended.

**Pre-pupal**: that stage in the larva just preceding the change to pupa.

**Prominent**: raised or produced beyond the level or margin: standing out in relief by color or otherwise: conspicuous.

**Pronotum**: the upper or dorsal surface of the prothorax.

**Prosternal**: belonging to the prosternum.

**Prosternal suture**: that suture of pro-thorax which separates the sternum front the pleural pieces.

**Prosternum**: the fore-breast: the sclerite between the fore-legs

**Protarsus**: the tarsus of the anterior leg.

**Pro-thorax**: the first thoracic ring or segment: hears the anterior legs but no wings: when free, as in Coleoptera. is usually referred to as "thorax" merely.

**Protuberance**: any elevation above the surface.

**Psammophilous**: living in sandy places.

**Pterygote**: wing bearing.

**Pubescent**: downy: clothed with soft, short, fine, closely set hair.

**Punctate**: set with impressed points or punctures.

**Punctiformis**: shaped like a point or dot.

**Punctulatus**: with small punctures.

**Puncture**: an impression like that made by a needle.

**Punctured**: marked with small, impressed dots.

**Pupa**: the intermediate stage between larva and adult; loosely applied for all orders, properly only for those with a complete metamorphosis: a pupa is obtect, when inclosed in a rigid case on which the members may or may not be outlined. It is liber, or free when the appendages are separately encased and there is no covering over the whole: see chrysalis.

**Puparium -ia**: in Diptera, the thickened larval skin within which the pupa is formed.

**Pupate, Pupation**: to become a pupa: the act of becoming a pupa.

**Rare**: seldom seen or found.

**Respiration**: breathing or taking breath: union of oxygen with tissues and liberation of carbon dioxide from same.

**Rugose -ous**: wrinkled: with irregular waved elevated lines.

**Sarothrum**: the basal joint of posterior tarsus in pollen gatherers: see metatarsus.

**Sclerite**: any piece of the body wall bounded by sutures.

**Sculpture**: the markings or pattern of impression or elevation on an elytra or other body surface.

**Sculptured**: a surface, when marked with elevations or depressions or both, arranged in some definite manner.

**Scutes**: the chitinous shields or plates on the segments of larvae.

**Secondary sexual characters**: features possessed by one sex but not the other, other than the differences of the reproductive organs themselves; e.g. color, size, shape, etc.

**Segment**: a ring or division bounded by incisions or sutures.

**Seriatim**: placed in longitudinal rows.

**Series**: a group of species, genera or families, arranged to show agreement in a common character which is not of sufficient importance to warrant the next higher division.

**Serrate**: saw-toothed, the teeth set toward one end.

**Seta -ae**: a pointed bristle or long stiff hair: slender, hair-like appendages.

**Setose -ous**: bristly or set with bristles.

**Side**: the lateral margin of the body.

**Slug**: in general, any larva that has a slimy viscid appearance, and the body closely applied to the food plant: more specifically, the larvae of certain saw-flies and of some Coleoptera.

**Smooth**: a surface without elevations or indentations.

**Sonoran faunal areas**: see upper and lower Sonoran.

**Species**: an aggregation of individuals alike in appearance and structure, mating freely and producing young that themselves mate freely and bear fertile offspring resembling each other and their parents: a species includes all its varieties and races.

**Spiculum**: a small spicule or thin, pointed process.

**Spiracle -cula**: a breathing pore: q.v.: in the plural the lateral openings on the segments of the insect body through which air enters the tracheae:= stigmata.

**Stadium -ia**: the interval between the molts of larvae:= instar q.v.: any one period in the development of an insect.

**Stage**: refers to the period of development; e.g. larval, pupal, etc.

**Sternellum**: the second sclerite of the ventral part of each thoracic segment frequently divided into longitudinal parts which may be widely separated.

**Sternite**: the ventral piece in a ring or segment.

**Stripe**: a longitudinal streak of color different from the ground.
**Sub-equal**: similar, but not quite equal in size, form or other characters.
**Subfamily**: a division of classification containing a group of closely allied genera; different from other allied groups, yet not so as to make a family series: opinionative, and ending in -inae.
**Subgenus**: a division within a genus, based upon a character not sufficient for generic separation; opinionative.
**Sulca**: grooves, furrows or channels: plural of sulcus.
**Sulcus**: a furrow or groove: a groove-like excavation.
**Super-family**: a division of classification less than an order, including a series of family groups more closely related to each other than to similar groups within the order: opinionative and ending in oidea: sometimes hardly different from suborder; but lower than suborder when both terms are employed.
**Suture**: a seam or impressed line indicating the division of distinct parts of body wall: the line of junction of elytra in Coleoptera.
**Tarsal**: relating to the tarsi, or feet.
**Tarsal lobes**: membranous appendages arising from the underside of the tarsal joints in some Coleoptera.
**Tarsus -i**: the foot; the jointed appendage attached at the apex of tibia. bearing the claws and pulvilli.
**Tawny**: a brownish yellow, like the color of a tanned hide [pale cadmium yellow + Indian red].
**Taxonomical**: systematic: relating to classification.
**Tegmina**: the thickened primaries serving as wing covers in Orthoptera.
**Teneral**: that state of the imago just after its exclusion from pupa or nymph, in which neither coloring nor clothing is fully developed.
**Thorax**: the second or intermediate region of the insect body, bearing the true legs and wings: made up of three rings, named in order, pro-, meso-, and meta-thorax: when the pro-thorax is free as in Coleoptera, Orthoptera, and Hemiptera, the term thorax is commonly used in descriptive work for that segment only.

**Tibia -ae**: the shank: that part of the leg articulated to the femur basally and which bears the tarsus at the distal end.

**Trachea -ae**: the spirally ringed breathing tube or tubes of insects.

**Translucent**: semi-transparent; admitting the passage of light but not of vision.

**Tribe**: a term of classification less than a subfamily: opinionative and ending in ini: but this is not universally adhered to.

**Tubercle**: a little solid pimple or small chitinous button: really a ring, which may or may not give rise to a seta.

**Tuberculate -ose**: formed like a tubercle: a surface covered with tubercles.

**Tubercule -ulum**: a small tubercle.

**Tuberculiform**: shaped like a pimple or tubercle.

**Tuberculose -ous**: covered or set with tubercles.

**Variola**: a deep, rounded impression with defined edges.

**Variolate -ose**: with large, rounded impressions like pock-marks.

**Ventral**: pertaining to the under surface of abdomen: in Diptera, that face of the leg which is inferior when laterally extended.

**Vermiform**: worm-shaped.

**Verrucose**: having little hard lumps or wart-like elevations.

**Vestigial**: small or degenerate: only a trace or remnant of a previously functional organ.

**Wax**: a ductile substance excreted by bees and other insects from glandular structures in various parts of the body, used in building cells or in forming a protective covering.

**Wing, Wings**: membranous reticulated organs of flight; one pair, the primaries, attached to the meso-thorax; the other, the secondaries, attached to the meta-thorax.

**Wing covers**: those parts of the chitinous cuticle of larvae, nymphs or pupae which cover the rudiments of the wings of the imago: the forewings of an imago when they are thicker than the hind wings and cover them when at rest: see elytra; tegmina.

**Xerophilous**: applied to species living in dry places.

www.ingramcontent.com/pod-product-compliance
Lightning Source LLC
Chambersburg PA
CBHW040933030426
42337CB00001B/2